How to Share GOOD NEWS

William George HARKEY

C.S.S. Publishing Co., Inc.

Lima, Ohio

HOW TO SHARE GOOD NEWS WITHOUT BEING OBNOXIOUS ABOUT IT

Library of Congress Cataloging-in-Publication Data

Harkey, William G. (William George), 1914-
   How to share the good news without being obnoxious about it.

   1. Witness bearing (Christianity)   2. Evangelistic work.   I. Title.
BV4520.H37   1988   248'.5   87-33191
ISBN 1-55673-030-6

8815 / ISBN 1-55673-030-6   PRINTED IN U.S.A.

Table of Contents

Introduction — 5

Chapter 1 — *"Oh, I Couldn't Possibly Do That!"* — 7

Chapter 2 — *"You Mean That's All I Have To Do?"* — 12

Chapter 3 — *"The Family Comes First — Doesn't It?"* — 26

Chapter 4 — *"Hi Neighbor — Hi Neighbor"* — 35

Chapter 5 — *It's True — Church Members Need Help* — 51

Chapter 6 — *Easy As Whistling While You Work* — 62

Chapter 7 — *The Sick Are Something Else!* — 73

Chapter 8 — *"I Found a Way to Rev Up Our Pastor"* — 90

Chapter 9 — *"Can I Bring an Outsider In?"* — 103

Chapter 10 — *You'll Never Witness Alone* — 116

Introduction

Our brave warriors, with large chain reference Bibles more imposing to some than 350 magnums, launch out on their soul-winning careers. The designated team partner knocks on the door while next to him his nervous friend prays silently, "Lord, please don't let anybody be home." No one answers the door, (whew). They think, "Maybe we should leave a tract and a note that we were here."

The evening produced two no-one-at-home calls. But, there was one person at home. A very domineering man. He proceeded to control the entire conversation with a boring tirade about some preacher who ran away with his organist. Then, he went into the story of his boyhood Sunday church school teacher who made him read aloud in class. He stated that he would never set foot in a church again as long as the choice was his to make. Our team leader meekly asked to pray before they left; the host patronizingly consented. During prayer, the other team member surreptitiously laid a tract on the coffee table.

They both then left, quite defeated in their mission. Sound familiar?

Don't misunderstand my point. In order to become effective in door-to-door evangelism, this kind of track record will dog the steps of all of us. Fear, anxiety, and disillusioning experiences will often be the fruit of the evening. The problem is that most witnesses, no matter how well-trained or sincere, give up and return to their usual routine on that particular night. They reason, and perhaps rightly so, that not everybody is cut out to do cold evangelism. So once again, they end up at home, flipping the television channels to their favorite program.

In my twenty-five years of pastoral experience, I have trained countless soul-winning teams. I have used Campus Crusade material; taught the "I Found It" campaign; used the Billy Graham course; and prepared people to work in the excellent "Evangelism Explosion" program developed by Dr. James Kennedy. But, I have found that no matter how good the material, or how excellent the training, with few exceptions, the ambitious once-a-week prodigies fall by the wayside after four to six weeks.

Everybody should be a witness, but not everybody in the same way. The longer I observe, the more I am persuaded that the key to leading someone to Jesus Christ is a gentle way-of-life method. Dr. William G. Harkey, my dear friend, and author of the book you now hold in your hands, has set forth in words and woven in spirit what every Christian leader would have liked to express, but seemingly could not. He has laid out for us all a "more excellent way."

In every chapter of this book, you will find yourself saying, "That's it . . . that is exactly how I have always felt it should have been done. Why, I can do that!"

This book is not a "soul-winning-made-easy" manual. It is rather a way of giving yourself to others in love, and that never comes easy. You will discover a crystal clear way of life set forth that all of us inwardly desire to live, sharing our love wherever we go. Dr. Harkey outlines to us how to live out our witness in a practical day-to-day walk which creates within those we meet a thirst to know this same Jesus that he knows.

Enter into a reading experience that may well alter your entire relational love experience toward others. I am satisfied that, if you will keep your heart open as you read the ensuing pages of this book, you may indeed become the gentle witness you have always desired to be.

D. Burdette Price, Director
Family Altar of the Air
International Radio Ministry
Battle Creek, Michigan

Chapter 1

"Oh, I Couldn't Possibly Do That!"

One of the most frightening experiences in the Christian life is to be asked to witness. Like 990 out of 1000 Christians, if you don't faint dead away, you end up:

1. Slipping into a state of silent panic;
2. Searching for some kind of an excuse;
3. Breaking out into a cold sweat;
4. Blurting out: "Oh, I couldn't possibly do that!"

As you struggle with your state of shock, you recall all the fears you've had about giving a testimony. You feel so inadequate. You might even experience anger at being asked. Yet, you know you should witness. God has commanded this of you. But, somehow, you just can't do it. Wow!

It's probably true that by nature you tend to be respectful and proper. Oh, there are certain occasions when you lose your bashfulness. But, on the whole, you bend over backward being considerate and civil. You strive not to intrude into anyone's life in an aggressive manner. You've probably come to the conclusion that witnessing is simply not for you, period.

It should be emphasized, at the start, that the majority of church members are very much like you. You love your Lord, but you hate to witness. You can't quite understand it, but are aware that some Christians are eager witnesses. Nevertheless, you cannot adjust to their styles. There are certain things you simply do not like. You notice that some Christian witnesses tend to be pushy. They violate others' privacy. They talk too much. You simply cannot accept this type of behavior. Nor can you change your personality to fit. God created you differently.

There is no reason to feel guilty or ashamed for the way

you are. We are all unique individuals. The Lord has good reason for creating each of us differently. It was the Lord who divided people into three personality groups: extroverts, ambiverts, and introverts. Extroverts are aggressive, outgoing persons. Introverts are shy and focused inwardly. Ambiverts are mixtures of these extremes. You are no more, nor no less, than the product of your God-given nature. Your gentle personality is hardly a flaw, but rather a divine claim to distinctiveness. If you feel you fall into the "shy" type category, you really have reason to rejoice. You can almost assuredly lay claim to being more creative, thoughtful, and conscientious. With these advantages, you can become, like thousands of others, effective — once you find a witnessing manner that fits your personality.

Your personality, the result of your genes, has become an advantage in our maturing society. Americans are changing physically, educationally, and religiously. The newer generations will live longer, be better educated, and expect more respect. In the church, newer understandings of the American people are changing methods of presenting the Gospel. Evangelists, pastors, and laypersons are adapting to these developments. The public opinion researcher, George Gallup, Jr., has discovered new facts about the beliefs and feelings of America's churched and unchurched. The impact of this research, as it becomes understood, is further changing witnessing approaches. It has revealed the presence of genuine faith in many of the unchurched. It emphasizes the need for change.

The Gospel has not changed. Regardless of the changes in society, the Gospel stands unaltered in any respect. Salvation through belief in Jesus Christ as Lord and Savior cannot be altered by any changing attitude of our society. Younger Americans, particularly, may incline toward new interpretations of sexual behavior, marriage, war, love, honesty, euthanasia, capital punishment, and a dozen other moral dilemmas.

Nevertheless, Scripture, as it relates to these problems, stands firmly.

Yet, the more America needs acceptable Christian witnessing, the less it is getting. Millions of sensitive Christians, like you and me, are discouraged by the old methods. We find strong-arm witnessing at odds with society's needs. We feel that increasing numbers of persons are being "turned off" by aggressive tactics. Many of the unchurched close both hearts and minds to abrasive witnessing approaches. Christians of all denominations are yearning for new concepts of witnessing. They are looking for new witnessing concepts that will find acceptance among the millions who now guard themselves against any approach.

Deep in your heart, though you are desperate to witness, you are frightened by all these circumstances. As you view many of today's witnessing procedures, you are deeply disturbed. Perhaps you're even angry. You have become aware of other Christian men and women — young and old, educated and hardly educated — who share this fear of current witnessing. In an effort to better understand evangelism, you might even have enrolled in a program at your church. But, try hard as you could, you really never made the grade, as prescribed. In view of all these experiences, you easily could reach the conclusion that witnessing just isn't for you. Or worse still, that something is wrong with your faith. Just the opposite is true.

If you were not a sensitive person, you would never entertain these negative thoughts. With some individuals, the whole problem is shed like water off a duck's back. For them no problem exists. But you are special. Very special. You are a type of personality that God wants to transform into a special witnessing. What you need is a new approach to witnessing — new procedures that are compatible with your personality — new sources of confidence. Both you and I have grave misgivings about the following:

Approaching total strangers, on an uninvited basis, to discuss the basics of Christianity. This is extremely difficult for the refined personality. It is considered a violation of privacy bordering on extremely bad manners.

Showing-off scriptural knowledge, based on the memorization of preselected Bible verses, which imitates "hard sell" commercial tactics. Distasteful to the sensitive Christian.

Arguing versus discussing occurs too often. It's particularly serious when the witness is overly concerned about specific denominational interpretations. This often offends ecumenical persons.

Using promotional devices, instead of teaching helps. Many of these "tricks" are not truly logical — or spiritual — and smack of Madison Avenue advertising techniques. Promotional trappings are rejected on the basis that they are used to "overwhelm" instead of teach.

Sending out teenage witnesses, usually because they are eager, and have recent convert-enthusiasm. This is a major miscalculation in the eyes of reserved Christians. They strongly react to the brashness of many youthful approaches.

Soliciting donations from strangers, for the Christian cause. With a few historic exceptions, such as the Salvation Army's Christmas kettles, this is a humiliating witness in the eyes of constrained Christians.

Lacking common civility in witnessing situations is inexcusable in the eyes of restrained Christians. God is love and love is the essence of good manners. If civility is lacking, the witness is self-defeating.

It is little wonder that you, and millions of other sensitive Christians, cry out, "Oh, I couldn't possibly do that!" when asked to witness. You are not saying "No!" to your Savior's command to go forth. You are, however, rejecting many questionable practices of today's lay evangelists. More than that, you are earnestly seeking new ways to witness. Ways which are more in tune with your sense of rightness.

Considerate Christians comprise the majority of believers. Often mistaken for being passive, most are deeply convicted and committed. They simply lack new guidelines for a caring, loving, lower-key witness. The traits identifying the shyer personality are frequently compassion, consideration, and selflessness.

If you know you are a considerate Christian, also know that you can become an unusually productive witness. Certainly, some types of aggressive witnessing are desirable for a minority of Americans. But, you should be encouraged that a gentle witness has a much wider audience. You can give a welcomed witness to a larger proportion of our population because they, like you, are of a gentle nature. Your own observation tells you that most Christians find aggressive witnessing objectionable. We must find ways to be more considerate, more caring, and more effective. This is the challenge.

The concept of the gentle witness may be the answer for you. It is scripturally based on 1 Thessalonians 2:7-8:

> *But we were gentle among you, even as a nurse cherisheth her children: So being affectionately desirous of you, we were willing to have imparted unto you, not the gospel of God only, but also our own souls, because ye were dear unto us.*

Paul did it. You and I can do it. We can give this type of a Pauline witness. It can come as easy as breathing. And, it will never fail because it is built on love — first, last, and always.

Never, never again will you need to say, "Oh, I couldn't possibly do that!" Rather, you can be quietly confident. You can be at peace with your Lord. You can look forward to the joy of witnessing. Most effectively.

Chapter 2

"You Mean That's All I Have To Do?"

To many people, the disclosure of the concept of the "gentle witness" might well remind them of the recent television show, *That's Incredible.* You may be amazed at its power, effectiveness, and simplicity. It will put within your grasp the means to quickly develop a dynamic Christian witness without becoming a biblical scholar; without applying aggressive behavior; without forcing unpleasant confrontations.

Once you come to an understanding of this type of testimony, you may well say to yourself, "I can't believe that's all there's to it!" In its simplicity you can find a new life of Christian service. And, it can add joy and zest to your every day. There are four areas of gentility that, when recognized, can make you an authentic witness for the rest of your life:

The Gentle *Being*
The Gentle *Attitude*
The Gentle *Caring*
The Gentle *Answer*

These four qualities may be used together, or separately, depending on the circumstances and your personal preferences. There are no hard and fast rules you have to observe. In practice, you can develop a highly individualistic approach to witnessing! There will be no one on earth who can interpret and execute the gentle approach exactly like you. Best of all, as a more reserved and quiet Christian, you will find the answer to your dilemma of obeying Christ's command to testify.

The first area to consider is:

The Gentle Being
Whether you feel you can't witness, whether you truly want

to witness, the fact remains that you *are* witnessing. There is nothing you can do about this. There is no escape. You are witnessing right now, and if you say you cannot witness, you are mistaken. Every Christian on earth, without conscious effort, is a visible example of Christ. You exert an influence on family, friends, even strangers. Understanding this most basic truth can give your life real meaning — right now.

Prove it by the Scriptures. They assure you that by being alive you are witnessing. And, you will continue to witness with your every breath. The apostle Paul boldly states this awesome truth in Philippians 1:20-21:

According to my earnest expectation and hope that in nothing I shall be ashamed, but that with all boldness, as always, so now Christ will be magnified in my body, whether by life or by death. For to me to live is Christ, and to die is gain.

It is hard to find a more mind-boggling two verses in all the Bible. If you are breathing, you are witnessing. Your presence in the world is used by the Holy Spirit to convince others of God's existence and power. This is your silent witness and, in many cases, your strongest witness. You don't have to utter a word to be effective.

The idea of innateness being able to communicate needs little argument. Few Americans can view the Statue of Liberty without getting a message. Or, could you glimpse the Pyramid of Cheops, covering thirteen acres and rising 500 feet in the air, without having your brain reel with impressions? If stone can witness by simply existing, how much greater can you, a silent Christian, witness. Your very being on this earth cries out that there is a God; there is a Christ; there is a Spirit. This is your silent statement. It is a miracle of the Holy Spirit.

Paul says that "Christ will be magnified in my body." This "enlargement of Christ" in our bodies is apparent to all. It becomes a witness when the Holy Spirit wants it to be so. Spiritual communications exist only when they are sent and received. You may be capable of originating testimony, but unless your message is received, there is no witness.

Who opens the receiver's mind and soul to the message? None other than the Holy Spirit. The world's finest advertising agency might create a brilliant witnessing commercial and broadcast it worldwide to billions of viewers. Yet, without the Holy Spirit opening the hearts of the viewers, it would mean nothing. In contrast, you, as a shy, retiring Christian, could set an example by your life which, if used by the Holy Spirit, would save a thousand souls.

Your personal effectiveness as a witness does not depend on your ability to talk, to teach, or to preach. It rests on the desire of the Holy Spirit. Your confidence should soar when you recognize that some of your bashful Christian friends have been used by the Holy Spirit in marvelous ways. Most shy Christians consider themselves unable to witness effectively. Yet, many have been given spiritual powers that outshine their aggressive friends. Above all, keep Luke 13:30 close to your heart:

And, behold, there are last which shall be first, and there are first which shall be last.

This Scripture is delightfully proved. In many Christian groups, timid souls may literally astound the others through their insights.

God uses the gifts of the evangelist, preacher, and scholar to bring the Gospel to millions. But hundreds of millions are being saved by the daily witness of "being" on the part of ordinary unsung Christians. It has been said that the Lord "whispers" to us. That he teaches quietly. As the unchurched and unsaved observe, the quiet Christian's "being" is more than enough to convince. This truth finds its ultimate expression in the words of the beloved hymn, "There's Life for a Look at the Crucified Lord."

But, the quiet Christian might ask, "Doesn't witnessing

involve words? Don't I have to speak out about God's plan of salvation?'' It might seem downright unfair that some persons have so little trouble in talking about God. They relish any kind of an opportunity to talk about Jesus. The larger the groups, the better. Evangelists and preachers yearn to address the largest of audiences. They show little nervousness when their television programs are being viewed by millions. That would paralyze most of us. Yet, a majority of ordinary church members find it almost impossible to speak out for Christ — even to family members! Does this fear doom our witness? Absolutely not. Even for the person who ''freezes'' when asked to testify, there is a wealth of witnessing possibilities.

Over many years I have treasured the axiom, ''One picture is worth a thousand words.'' I believe that the ''picture of my life'' speaks volumes. Not a thousand, but perhaps millions of words over my lifetime. My witness is then not words, but life itself. Most importantly, this witness of ''being'' creates more conviction than spoken testimony. I know that what I am convinces more than what I say. If you're worried about your lack of ability to talk about Jesus, forget it. If you never spoke one word of testimony, your ''being,'' your life, would be your witness. By living, you are witnessing right now. Rejoice in this strong witness of your being. You are being used by God!

The Gentle Attitude

Your silent witness of ''being'' finds more support in your attitudes. Your attitudes are observable testimony that influence others. Attitudes about yourself, your neighbors, and your God, touch lives with a force that is hard to believe. The attitude of our Savior — so soft, yet so strong — as captured in the beloved old hymn, illustrates the point:

Softly and tenderly Jesus is calling
Calling for you and for me

See, on the portals He's waiting and watching
Watching for you and for me.

— Will L. Thompson

Most hard-hitting Christians prefer a more aggressive attitude. They "press" in their meetings with the unsaved. They forcefully seek immediate decisions. Certainly, under some circumstances, this type of effort is needed. Nevertheless, Christ is pictured accurately as "waiting and watching." In Scripture, he is reported to have been reticent to meet with the crowds. He was at his evangelistic best on a one-to-one basis. Nowhere in the Scriptures is he depicted as a master salesman, a spellbinding preacher, a sparkling personality. His life sets the example for you and for me. He let his loving, caring attitude speak with authority. He never seemed to force decisions. He spoke, when asked, in parable logic. He asked questions, allowing the Holy Spirit to work in the hearts of his listeners. His were the attitudes that you, and I, as gentle Christians, can duplicate.

History records the fact that nations which were considered the most civilized were usually well-behaved. National attitudes of graciousness and humility were benchmarks of their civility. When a person begins to live life around these attitudes, a silent witness demands attention and consideration. If you and I would win a respect for our witness, we must first win the praise of others for how we live. If a person can look at you and say, "He is a fine man, or she is a wonderful woman," it indicates a successful witness. The silent witness of your attitude makes a convincing statement for your Christianity. You can accomplish this winning with a minimum effort of thoughtfulness and love.

This witness will be fruitful only if it is honest. If solely a gesture, it becomes hollow and meaningless. You can't fake an attitude for long. If you are found to be an imposter, the end result is disaster. Your graciousness, politeness, and consideration of others, if only for show, will deserve, and get, rejection. You will win the respect of others only if you honestly respect others.

You and I have a serious challenge in facing the unchurched and unsaved with the respect they deserve. We note that a great many otherwise good Christians assume a superior posture to the non-Christian. It seeps through in numerous and subtle ways. The worst manifestation occurs among the self-righteous. Their good works loom so large in their minds that their desirable self-esteem turns into intolerable pride. To judge persons only by their good works might be human, but it is not the way God looks at the lost. This lamentable arrogance of some Christians, though they may not admit that it exists, short-circuits their effectiveness. In the parable of the prodigal, the greater love was shown to the sinning son. Our love and respect, too, should be showered on the non-Christian. To the non-righteous.

To be true to yourself and honest to others is an attitude well worth cultivation. There exists a compatibility between the gentle Christian and these two attitudes. In the realization of the truth that you are a sinner saved by grace is born an honesty that appeals. As you live your life, you constantly are being evaluated. In a sense, you are "on stage" all the time, being judged. If, like "Honest Abe" Lincoln, you earn a reputation of being trustworthy, your witness will be blessed.

It's not always easy to be honest with others. Little white lies are so convenient. If you would remain honest, some situations demand you either be silent, or walk away from the problem. This is not a "cop out." It is an honest means of allowing God to work out the problem rather than us. Many situations might challenge you not to act but to pray. Paul states that reconciliation is from God. Christians forget that it is not the persuasive power of man that results in understandings. It is an honest attitude that openly admits and allows for this miracle.

A final leg in building a witnessing attitude is the quality of enthusiasm. A triangle of *civility — honesty — enthusiasm* becomes the three-part attitudinal structure that protects your witness. Enthusiasm often escapes us because it is somehow mistaken for an undesirable use of emotion. Also, you might feel enthused about your Christian beliefs, but shun an outward show, because you feel it is not in good taste. You might confuse enthusiasm with fanaticism or bigotry, attitudes which are not acceptable. Yet, the lack of some degree of enthusiasm can mar an otherwise appealing attitude. Nobody appreciates the person who cannot become enthusiastic. With little effort, you can develop your enthusiasm and improve your acceptance.

One definition of enthusiasm relates it to inspiration from a divine power. Who is in a better position to become enthusiastic than a Christian walking close to God? Every morning I repeat, and so can you, a phrase which is my daily tonic, guaranteed to generate enthusiasm; it is Psalm 118:24: "This is the day which the Lord has made; let us rejoice and be glad in it." Repeating these words can help you "have a good day!" If you face every day being glad because it is the Lord who made it, you will become the kind of a person that people like to be around.

Once you're powered by this thought for the day, turn to just one more verse: Philippians 1:21: "For me to live is Christ, and to die is gain." What a thought! First, you realize you can be glad and rejoicing for the day; then, whether in this day you live or die, all is goodness and gain. How wonderful. How great. You and I can own an enthusiasm not based on genes, psychology, or events; but solidly on the promises of God. Talk about reasons for being enthusiastic!

Your enthusiasm, based on the word of God, can become the power of your personality. It will shine out, bathing persons in the light of the Spirit. The ultra rays of the Spirit will be absorbed by those around you. They will feel better. Like laughter, enthusiasm is contagious. Forget being solemn, somber, or grave. Christ came to bring joy to the world. Your Christian enthusiasm is proof that you believe him and want others to share the joy.

Expressing these attitudes is comfortably non-aggressive. It is like wearing clothes that quietly attract. The wearing of these attitudes is a passive witness. It requires no abrasive, aggressive, or overt action. For all of their passiveness, these three attitudes have power as testimony. It becomes impossible to shy away from gentle attitudes by using the excuse that they are too difficult to perform. The qualities of *civility — honesty — enthusiasm* can be mastered by all. As you make them part of your life, you will become more Christ-like. Like our Savior, you will be influencing others to seek you out, to ask you for help, to open themselves to your love.

The Gentle Caring

As a caring but considerate Christian, you lean over backwards not to intrude. You have a sense of awe and wonderment about spiritual matters. You are careful not to push your personal interpretations of Scripture. You are inclined to resist forcing yourself on others. You harbor a deeply ingrained distaste to "meddle," preferring to respect others' dignity and right to privacy. It is possible for you, under these conditions, to express love and caring in a soul-saving manner? Positively!

Care is a healing balm to be applied with intelligence. No help results unless there first exists a need. Better still if the need is a crying for help. If you use this qualification — the presence of a genuine need — your caring will be without fear or embarrassment. Your caring witness will blossom once you meet the real needs of your neighbor.

Do you think the Good Samaritan was embarrassed when he helped the bandit's victim? For him, as it can be for you, caring for one in real need was the most natural thing in the world. To bind the victim's wounds, give him water, and see that he would be sheltered did not involve the least embarrassment, just love. In this parable, the Scripture emphasizes practical assistance. The needs could not be resolved through spiritual counseling. The Scripture points out that the bandages, the drink of water, the offer of financial assistance were the required witnessing tools. While it does not say so in the story, you and I can only imagine what great satisfaction the Samaritan had after helping. We would also like to think of him as an ordinary being, not steeped in theology, overwhelmed with compassion when he saw a need crying out for help.

You'll soon find yourself becoming aware of the real needs of people around you. The need does not have to be one of life or death. It could be a tiny need that looms like a mountain — small needs can often assume life-threatening proportions. The need for a small Christmas gift during the season, the need for transportation of the sick, handicapped, or indigent, the need for a little extra money to help an unemployed neighbor, even the need for a warm handshake at a particularly tough time during someone's day. None of these needs are earth-shattering. Yet, in the world of witnessing, their solutions demonstrate the love of Christ shining through.

In the automobile industry there is a slogan that increases in importance as the years roll by. It is simply, "Care Will Save Your Car." Caring for people is identical. Once you discover that something in a person's life needs caring, attend to it. Promptly. There is not a person alive who would resent help to meet a need that was being overlooked. Care, expressed in practical ways, and used by the Holy Spirit, can figure in the saving of souls. Car care may relate to tires, the engine, or the body; in a person, it may be food, clothing, or shelter. Meeting the practical needs of others is the life blood of a good witness. It is the testimony of love expressed not just vocally, but tangibly.

Whenever you think of acquaintances, be amply curious about their needs. What they need — a word of comfort, food, clothing, or shelter — perhaps they just need to talk. From this "need list," select the one (or two) you are in a position to satisfy. Then promptly address the need; supply what is lacking. Do not hesitate to bring over that bowl of hot soup, suggest you help with yard work, offer to drive, invite to a church affair, or help find answers to more personal problems. When you supply a need, you become God's partner on earth.

You need not worry if your help is not accepted. Perhaps there is good reason. But, be sure your offer will not be forgotten. Some types of financial and tangible help, to certain very proud persons, might be declined. If the offer is made in a sensitive way, there need be little embarrassment for either party. Look on any rejection positively. It might well pave the way for later friendships.

There are other ways of caring and sharing. Expressing your concern through organization work allows you to witness in a detached fashion. Your church continually needs you. As a singer, musician, usher, officer, or helping hand, your witness will count. Working with the Salvation Army, the Red Cross, the hospital auxiliary, or scores of other fine organizations is a visible testimony. Your job can be in the public eye, or in the background. Either way, it will count as your witness. As a big plus, organizational witness results in making new friends, opening up opportunities for personal caring.

Caring always opens the door to answer questions about your faith. How easy it is when someone asks you to share your beliefs. It is crucial to the shy Christian to have the initiative come from the other person. Questions like: "Do you attend church?", "Are you a Christian?", or, "What church do you go to?" can be answered in a word or two. This might seem like small witness to you. Remember, however, the inquirer is comparing your answers with your actions. Then, the Holy Spirit willing, these evidences can spark a conversion or commitment. Your caring is love, and love never fails. Love is stronger than words; than knowledge; than wisdom.

The Gentle Answer

The fourth facet of the gentle witness proved its effectiveness in the life of Jesus. Much of his personal witness was in response to questions. Kings, beggars, disciples, saints and sinners alike came to him with problems. Humanity was sick, seeking answers. As it was in his days — so it is in ours. Today's humanity is seeking answers to age-old problems. From impending war, to the relationship between church and state, to the means of personal salvation, the questions keep coming. Most of us can handle only a few elementary questions. But, we can give these answers with love. This becomes the strength of our witness.

Our strength is not in challenging others. Our God-given sensitive natures are better suited for listening, not talking, for comforting, not confronting; for helping, not harassing. God has given us an ability to assist, console, and advise when and if we are needed. This we can do confidently. The Holy Spirit is always present when we are asked questions. You may feel that some of the answers you give to spiritual queries are inadequate. Even incorrect. But, there is little cause for worry. Answers given in love, and coming straight from the heart, will be used by God in ways beyond our understanding.

A little child, your own or your neighbor's, may ask the most fundamental of questions. How often have we heard, "Mommy, will I to go Heaven?" Your husband or wife might inquire, "What did you think of the sermon this morning?" Or, a new neighbor seeks helpful suggestions, "Does your family attend a church?" The answers you give to everyday questions like these constitute the very heart of your witness.

Answers from friends are the most believable. We should never under-estimate the witness that comes from the pulpit, the radio, or the TV tube. But, for generating believability and conviction, nothing is stronger than a witness from someone close. When two persons are sharing the same slice of life, at the same time, and in the same way, there exists a measure of extra believability. This is why peer pressure is so strong. And, it is also the reason for becoming friends while you witness.

When friends ask for answers to spiritual questions, they do not expect, need, nor want profound replies. What they seek are simple answers, based on experience, and given in love. You may not be able to supply answers without the expertness of a minister. Nevertheless, your experiences as a layperson might well be much more convincing. The power of a real-life experience is impossible to ignore. In a recent television panel of top economists, in Washington, D.C., no agreement could be reached on whether inflation was persisting. Scholarly arguments flew fast from both sides. Finally, a housewife in the audience got the mike and said, "Last month a dozen eggs and a pound of butter cost me $2.79 at my supermarket. Yesterday, I paid $3.19 for the same items." The impact from that shopper's experience was devastating.

If you do not know the answer to a question asked you — admit it. You need never be ashamed of not knowing. But you will be embarrassed if you try to "fake" an answer and are found out. Most persons feel they are being treated honestly when ignorance is admitted. They are asking the questions, in the first place, because they themselves do not know. Unlike a professional minister or lay evangelist, you are not expected to be an expert. Your advice is sought because an honest reply is expected to be given. This is your important advantage for it gives strength to your witness. You should feel confident under any circumstances.

When you are asked a spiritually-related question, it is the inquirer who is asking the favor. Whether you answer the question satisfactorily or not, you remain in control. This is a more advantageous position than that usually experienced by aggressive witnesses. The Christian who "comes on strong," is, in reality, saying "I don't think you believe as I do and I'm going to show you why I'm right!" How much better is the answer, "I don't know whether I can answer your questions about the faith, but I'll be happy to tell you what I believe!"

Your preparation for answering spiritual questions can be accomplished privately. Reading your Bible, attending Bible study groups, and church worship are recommended. This will build your spiritual confidence. It will firmly "establish in your own mind" your personal faith. More than anything else, when you have a firm faith, answering questions is not all that difficult. Your personal interpretation of Christ as Lord and Savior is a matter between you and God. Your faith is the result of private truths that the Holy Spirit has implanted in your heart. No two faiths in Christ are exactly alike any more than any two people are identical. In giving your answers, it is well to inform the inquirer that your answers are just your personal understanding. Don't expect people to accept your interpretation of Christianity without question. They must decide for themselves, with the help of the Holy Spirit, on their own private paths to eternal life.

It becomes apparent that each of us must develop a personal tolerance toward the private beliefs of others. You and I will be enriched if we "respect to be respected!" All struggle to find their individualistic ways to believe in God, some more than others, to be sure. In answering questions, in the kindest way, respect for the views of the other person is imperative. No matter how difficult, it is only by being genuinely respectful and understanding of a diverse or opposite viewpoint that we can even begin to communicate. Every belief has some value. Every life is God.

You need never fear you will lack questions to answer. Your very being, your attitudes, and your caring for others will identify you as a person who will listen to problems. People with sensitive questions don't seek answers from aggressive individuals. They shy away because they fear for their privacy and their cherished beliefs. They tend to look for non-threatening persons. As you live life in gentle fashion, there will be one opportunity after another to deal with delicate questions. The word will spread that you are one who, perhaps, can be helpful. In today's world, with a myriad of personal problems, you will be sought out as a person who cares to give answers.

There is small doubt that the great commission — bringing the faith to all nations — is being accomplished. The impact of worldwide television and radio, of spectacular ministries, of scholarly works from renowned seminaries will be felt. Yet, more far reaching than all of this is the twenty-four hour a day, seven days a week, presence of millions of ordinary Christians. They are always available, always caring, always sharing the faith. This constitutes a mighty force, used by the Holy Spirit, for the redemption of lost souls.

As a gentle witness, realize that you are one of the most important communicators of the Gospel. Never, never, never feel unequal to those who are more flambuoyant, more verbal, more accomplished. You are part of that human foundation of believers that is present, at all times, to help all the sheep, in all the flocks of God's children. Without you, and millions like you, the churches would be empty. The multi-media evangelistic extravaganzas would be cancelled. The basic strength of Christian nations would cease to exist. You are the Christ-like kind of Christian that is witnessing — and winning.

For Him.

Chapter 3

"The Family Comes First — Doesn't It?"

Suppose the Lord came to you one day, and said, "I'll grant your family any wish you want, just ask me." It is almost a foregone conclusion that you would ask, "Lord, I wish that every member of my family would become a Christian, and that we would all stay together in eternity!"

It's so true that "blood is thicker than water." Whenever the going gets tough, the family comes first. God has made us so. He has made the family, to quote one source, "The most instinctive, fundamental social or mating group in man and animal, especially the union of man and woman through marriage and their offspring; parents and their children." The family consists of servants serving the needs and wants of each other. In human society, no other social unit has proved as effective. And, in society, the Christian family has the potential of being the most nearly perfect of all social units.

Concern for your mother, father, sister, brother, wife, husband, daughter, son, and even further-removed family is one of the most compelling facts of your life. Sharing blood, bone, genes and common life, the family comes first. Witnessing to your family should be easy. Right? Wrong! It just might be the hardest job you've ever tackled. But, believe it, there are ways.

While you may take the saying, "Familiarity breeds contempt," with serious doubts, it does contain a tad of truth. In the family, your whole life is an open book. Your good points and strengths are appreciated, to be sure. But, unlike outside the family, you cannot hide your weaknesses and shortcomings. Marriage counselors often warn, "You never know a person until you live with him or her." How true this is! Few people, outside your immediate family, know your private habits, your physical hang-ups, your rock-bottom attitudinal approach to life. The fact that these "civilized secrets" are everyday reading to family members poses a witnessing problem of considerable challenge.

Interestingly, those who are P. K.s (Preacher's Kids) have family experiences more contrasting than most. They admire their father and mother in the pulpit, at the study podium, and mixing with the congregation. But, they are dismayed when parents are at odds with each other, disciplining the children, struggling with health, money, and congregational problems. For most of us, sad to say, it takes too many years before we comprehend our parent's true worth. But, somewhere along the line comes a blessed revelation: that in spite of their flaws, they are truly wonderful. We, then, earnestly pray that they will forgive us our many shortcomings.

Families share the private lives of their members. That is one disadvantage of the family — there's no privacy! Because you are known so intimately, how can you be assured they will accept your witness, being aware of your shortcomings? The answer can be found in another answer. How can God accept you, being fully aware of all your shortcomings? The answer is simple — love! He so loved that he gave his Son, Jesus, as a sacrifice for you. You, with all of your sins! If you, as a sinner, are loved and accepted by God, how can you fear not being loved and accepted by your family? Neither God, nor your family, will appreciate your wrongdoing. But, they'll love you for your rightdoing. This can be your family witness. The effort to be a Christian example to your family, is not nearly so easy as witnessing to strangers. However, it promises the great reward of saving and keeping the family together — eternally.

Another sizable witnessing disadvantage is to occupy a favored position in the family. Certain privileges affix themselves to the father, mother, first child, youngest, oldest, most attractive, most brilliant, etc., etc. Taking undue advantage, by placing too much importance on these favorable conditions, is easy to do. This becomes devastating to the other family members.

Still another family hurdle is the natural existence of sibling and parental rivalries. Parents may vie for the affection of particular children and cause unhappiness. In like manner, some children press hard for greater attention from mother, father, or favorite brother or sister. All these familial conditions, if present, make it more difficult to carry on an acceptable witness inside the family circle. "Wow," you might say, "witnessing to the family is impossible!"

Before you throw in the towel, let's look at the bright side. Here are some factors that are encouraging:

1. Your family is a group of related people held together by love. This love extends to all members — you included. They will look upon your witness with love.

2. In your family, the small are great, and the great are small. Whatever your position in the family, you not only receive love, but also respect. Believe it.

3. Your family is the place where you can grumble the most while, at the same time, be treated the best. Where else can you find this fortunate circumstance?

4. In your family you are secure; all its members may not agree with you, but they'll protect you. How wonderful to be shielded.

5. Your family will be honest with you; there is no need for them to be hypocritical. They'll keep you "on the ball."

6. Your family will be encouraging to your efforts. They'll meet you more than half way if you're reasonable and respectful.

7. Your family will welcome your *being, attitude, caring, answering* and work it into their lives, in their way, in their time. Be patient.

The family is the last place for an aggressive, arrogant, and authoritative manner. You have probably heard of examples where fanatically-inclined converts have not only split the family, but destroyed their testimony. If you place self above other family members, you are destined to fail. When you put the family first, good results multiply — one after another after another!

If there is one conclusion to be reached about witnessing to your family, it is probably this: the family is the worst, and the best, of all witnessing opportunities. The good news is that you, yourself, have it within your power to make it the best. Courteous witnessing will make your job easier. There are good reasons, and solid proof, that this is so. Consider how these four basic approaches smoothly interact inside the family:

The Gentle Being — In the Family.

If you are like most of us — a kind being — the other members of the family will know this. They will be more gentle to you, simply because they recognize you dislike harshness and violence. Oh, they might forget, now and then, but their "being" will tend to be similar to yours.

What a headstart a gentle being has. You will be respected, even when your views differ from the rest of the family. Your gentle being opens doors, and minds, that are shut tight to others. It's great to realize that gentle people are not the "losers" in God's plan. You can have a quiet confidence. It will help win over the family.

You should be careful with this confidence. To allow assurance to become arrogance would be sad. In days past, one favorable description of a man was, "He's the strong, silent type." For men and women, the ability to be self-assured, without talking too much, is an asset. As a gentle, quiet, assured being, your mere physical presence within the family can mean first, a productive life for you; and, second, a major source of satisfaction for your family.

This quality of being — just being — seems not to be fully understood or appreciated. Being is not mere appearance. It becomes a projected image of what lies behind the outward appearance. Einstein wrote that his work was to probe "beyond the appearance of the facts." Meaning of being is far beyond appearance of being. It almost becomes a spiritual communication between two persons. In a sense, it is ESP — extrasensory perception. And, in the Christian realm, it is aided by the power of the Holy Spirit.

The gentle being is you; the gentle being is recognized by your family; the gentle being is used by the Holy Spirit. Let it be a wonder-working witness in your household.

The Gentle Attitude — In the Family.

As gentle being evolves to gentle attitude, more family witness progress can be made. The goals to shoot for are threefold: loving in its approach, gracious in its application, and attractive to all. This is not easy. But, it is attainable. Before trying to reach these limitations:

1. You will never be perfect.
2. You can't please everybody.

Because the family is the closest-knit of social units, your attitudes are readily apparent to all. Reactions toward the most insignificant, or most important, happenings become family business. You will be constantly judged on the basis of your attitudes. These judgments will either help or harm your acceptability as a Christian example.

The closer your attitudes duplicate those recorded about our Savior, the better will be your witness. While it won't be easy, closer study of his life will point the way. In developing good attitudes, you are fortunate to be of a gentle temperament. Christ's attitudes, while on earth, were ones of softness and tenderness. You are already inclined this way. He will forgive you if you occasionally react like Peter, and let your temper get the best of you. Nevertheless, your gentle personality will enable you to more easily walk through life "In His footsteps." You can, much more readily, resist the temptation to lash out in anger. Your "born in" peace-loving personality resists the temptation to be aggressive, abrasive, or authoritative. With God's help, your gentleness can build attitudes that will influence the family to follow him.

The Gentle Caring — In The Family.

This should come naturally. It springs from a feeling that is inborn in most families. There exists a natural desire to protect and care for each other, to preserve family members' well-being at all costs. In the first instance, mother and father love each other. Then their love develops a caring for the children. As life progresses, it ends with the children caring, not only for their own offspring, but for their own parents. As old families phase out, the new ones begin. Quality of caring continues to grow in the family circle where love abounds.

Many times, the first signs of caring come when a brother or sister needs help, from forces outside the immediate family. Brother may be threatened by a bully at school, and you come to the rescue. Or sister can't walk as fast as the rest of the family, so you pick her up and carry her. Caring is born in these simple situations. It increases in importance as long as two or more family members are alive. Strangely, some of the most indelible caring memories are those which occur during our youth.

As the family matures, caring becomes more involved. The younger family members need care in coping with the very basics of life — putting on clothes, eating, attending to personal cleanliness. As time passes, whole new ranges of caring become obvious. There is help with schoolwork, help in learning games and sports, advice about getting along with others. For the older family members, the spectrum of caring enlarges to embrace all of life. Help with children, assistance in home chores, social guidance, even financial assistance are all frequent caring needs. There is no shortage of caring needs. This is your opportunity.

The value of meeting material needs is always stressed. While spiritual communication between family members is important, caring through concrete deeds is vital. Tangible help in any situation, gifts at all appropriate times, a supplying of whatever is needed to make life easier — this is concrete caring. Your caring inside the family circle, as expressed in meeting material problems must never be underestimated. If you love your family, you'll care deeply. Your offers to be of help — no matter how far from the spiritual — create appreciation for your beliefs.

One problem that all of us face is the necessity to respect the opinions of other family members. As seriously as you might disagree with parents, children, or other family members, it becomes a must not to elevate your disagreement to argument. Nobody ever wins an argument. While in our case, our more sensitive temperaments help us, there is still need for control. Caring demands control; control of your feelings, the expression of which might cause deep scars. Your caring must be careful and considerate to be constructive.

The Gentle Answer — In The Family.

This is a little different from answering questions from strangers. There is one added word of caution. If you love your family like most of us, you forget that familiarity tends to make us careless. You might be guilty, in giving your answers, of a lack of real respect. Somehow, in our family relationships, we take liberties we would never dream of with strangers. It is so easy, knowing the intimate "secrets" of the life of parents, brothers, or sisters, to answer their questions in a more insensitive vein. You'll know when you make this mistake. It will bother you.

If your family is not closely-knit, it might take time before they ask serious questions. The first questions asked usually spring up from curiosity and are impersonal. They can be answered easily and frankly. At this point, you may find it desirable not to probe into your family member's personal beliefs. Just tell them of yours. This may be hard if their questioning tinges on ridicule. While you might struggle to respect their viewpoints, they may not be so kind. But hang in there. Don't lose control. Realize that they simply do not understand. Treat them with respect if they try to ridicule your explanations. Sometimes they sheepishly will come back to you for more information. Keeping your control pays off — big!

Is it worth it, you might ask? It appears that all the effort is one-sided. You are asked by family members to explain your faith, and when you do, you may be subjected to ridicule. This is the price you pay to seize a golden opportunity. How can you put a price on being asked to help your parents, brother, sister, son, or daughter come to a better understanding of God. When this happens, and it almost always will, the angels in heaven will sing, and you will feel the touch of the Master. There is no joy that can begin to compare with that of helping lead one of your family to a saving faith, or a committed life, in the Lord. It can be done simply — by answering questions!

Patience and control, simply as words, are not very exciting. But, control and patience, as qualities, are forces of supernatural strength. Through them you can stand fast in your faith and wait for the family to come to you, to seek your answers. Like Christ, you can watch and wait. Sooner or later you will be asked to witness. What a witness it can be as brother or sister, son or daughter, perhaps even mother or father, open up their needs to you. The Holy Spirit can use this surrender of a resisting will to implant faith and hope as in no other type of a situation. To have a part in this godly miracle is unimaginable joy.

Whatever your degree of gentle witness to your family, whatever testimony you build, you cannot do anything but succeed if you use the cement of love:

Love suffereth long
Love is kind
Love envieth not
Love vaunteth not itself
Love is not puffed up
. . . and if in your heart you believe "The Family Comes First,"
know that, in your Gentle Witness:
"Love Never Faileth!"

Chapter 4

"Hi Neighbor — Hi Neighbor!"

If you are like most of us, you have had neighbors whom you will never forget. They are, in *Reader's Digest* language, "Unforgettable Characters." A man who typified this description lived two doors away from me in a Chicago suburb. He was icy. I was friendly. A curt "Hi" was all I could ever get out of him. One day, I noticed him in his backyard, practicing his golf swing. It was almost professional. It was beautiful.

Being a terrible golfer, I quickly sensed a chance to "break the ice." I would get my neighbor to give me his advice. I strolled over to his fence with, "Hi neighbor, would you mind giving an old duffer a few tips?" In a matter of minutes he was coaching me like a club pro. Within weeks, we were teeing off together. We quickly went from bad neighbors to good friends. Around Christmas time, would you believe, we were sharing our Christian concepts. It took a little time. It was worth the time — and then some.

You and I are more than a little concerned whether our neighbor knows Christ as Lord and Savior. What we need are some of the most tactful, yet effective, ways to interest neighbors in spiritual matters. People with our kind of personalities would never "jump in with both feet." Nor would we confront our neighbor with pointed questions. Nor, would we pursue our viewpoint until we forced some kind of a spiritual decision.

As courteous neighbors, we would develop a friendly relationship first. Try to find activities which you have in common. Perhaps you can enjoy conversation about sports, the job, yard work, or find common ground relating to family, shopping, hobbies or other interests. Friendship becomes the first, and foremost, goal in witnessing to neighbors. Best of all, developing friendships is free from embarrassment, and usually a pleasure.

Neighbor-friendships grow to the point where you can be of practical assistance. The help may be only in small ways. If my neighbor is sick, I bring hot soup! If lonely, I visit! If having a birthday, I send a card. These acts of civility are important love deeds. Through them, it is possible for you to build friendship to the point where your neighbor will "open up" to you.

It is so true that "What you do speaks louder than what you say." If you want to "speak the loudest" to your neighbor, make sure you "do." As these love deeds pile up, they overcome obstacles to friendship. When the proper time comes, your neighbor will feel free to ask you spiritual questions. The questions will be asked you because you have won not only acceptance, but trust. By the time you are asked to witness, it comes easily. You are simply asked to give honest answers. As you do, you witness. Wonderfully!

Neighborly witness starts with love deeds. Your neighbors look at what you "do" as the real test of your love and concern for them. If one picture is worth a thousand words, one love deed is worth a thousand pictures. To express your love with a deed fulfills God's royal commandment, "Thou shalt love the Lord thy God with all thine heart, soul, and mind, and thy neighbor as thyself." The importance of your neighbor is second only to God and self. Loving your neighbor is not a matter of morality. It is obedience to a commandment.

Decide on those neighborly love deeds that would be of greatest help. The following list includes some suggestions which might be helpful:

Extend a cheerful "Good Morning" every day.
Invite neighbors in for coffee or a visit.
Engage them in conversation whenever feasible.
Plan to go visiting or shopping together.
Give luncheons or dinners if possible.
Entertain them if you are musical.

Introduce them to your friends and acquaintances.
Show genuine concern for their physical well being.
Help and encourage them when they are ill.
Visit them regularly if they're hospitalized.
Provide transportation if needed.
Work out baby-sitting, if you're able.
Recognize birthdays and anniversaries.
Loan or borrow tools, implements, etc.
Offer gardening help if you can.
Assist in helping make repairs.
Exchange food, utensils, recipes, albums, books.
Bring over desserts, special dishes, other foods.
Go fishing, golfing, bowling together.
Give them spare books, periodicals, or films.
Attend shows, concerts, special events with them.
Help whenever an extra hand is needed.
Recommend professional people, if asked.
Discuss school, social, and community interests.
Keep a watchful eye on their home and property.
Listen to them, above all else.

This list of love deeds seems obvious. You most certainly can lengthen it, shorten it, or in other ways tailor it to meet the needs of your neighbors. You will know how to "zero in" on exactly the helps that are most needed at any particular time. If a new baby has just arrived, if the neighbor is leaving on a trip, if illness or death hits a family, common sense will dictate what to do. Certain people appreciate specific helps: the person who loves to cook cherishes new recipes; the mechanically-minded relish fix-up short-cuts; the sports person appreciates any exceptional news about the games. This tailoring of love deeds shows the extra caring that enhances your witness.

While love deeds open hearts to spiritual matters, you should never consider this to be their primary purpose. The deed's the thing. The love involved is agape love. No return should be expected, no reward is required. The love of the deed is its own reward. Once accomplished it fulfills the commandment of loving your neighbor. You need not worry if the love deed misfires, if it becomes inappropriate, or even if it is not wholly acceptable. You act in love, and love never fails.

When you offer a glass of water, be sure it is to slake thirst. If you invite a beggar in for food, the reason should be to satisfy hunger. If you extend a helping hand, its purpose is to be of comfort. Your love deeds should stand by themselves; never to be performed to achieve a secondary purpose. If you spend a lifetime loving your neighbors, and do not get a single opportunity to point them to their Savior, your love deeds are not in vain. In obeying the commandment to love God, yourself, and your neighbor, you are witnessing. Who can discern how the Holy Spirit will use any love deed?

When there are no strings attached, love deeds are the essence of a committed Christian's life. If you expect personal benefits for your love deeds, you are playing a game. A game, incidentally, that you hope to win. To love to be loved is not love. Pure response to a neighbor's need does not expect a return. A love deed is a response to a cry for help. The person helped should not be expected to pay you back in any way. When God "so loved the world" he demanded nothing in return. Love gives, it does not get.

Whether neighbors are rich or poor, disagreeable or likable, white or black, God asks us to love them. It is God who gives us our neighbors. They reside near us to become objects of our love. They test our brand of Christianity. Stephen C. Neill put it beautifully in his work, "Who Is My Neighbor":

Our friends are the people we choose; usually friends are the same sort of people as ourselves. My neighbor is the man whom I do not choose; he is the man who God gives to me. He is the man who happens to sit opposite to me in the train; he is the clerk who works at the desk next to mine. I have no right to say he is of no concern of mine, because, if I am a Christian, I know he is the man whom God has given to me.

What a thought! God knows us, picks out particular neighbors for each of us, and then plants them near us. If your neighbor is like you, a Christian, wonderful! If your neighbor is a nominal Christian, wonderful! If your neighbor is unsaved and unchurched, wonderful! All have been given you by God, and can become the objects of your love deeds. They are your reasons for caring and sharing. On them you can focus your love. They can become one of your most important reasons for living. In the words of an old song, they become the "objects of your affections" to give you purpose and joy.

You cannot experience this joy of loving and doing for your neighbors without paying a price. It is a small price. But, it looms large in the minds of many Christians. The price is involvement. Today, you often hear the statement, "I didn't want to get involved." Accident victims are left to die in their wrecks; persons mugged are ignored by passersby; brutal crimes go unpunished, all because somebody didn't want to get involved. The parallel exists when a neighbor's need is ignored for fear of personal involvement. How can you justify a "hands off" attitude when your neighbor needs help?

In today's world, this is not a simple problem. It is complicated by our laws, courts, and legal procedures. Persons who have tried unsuccessfully to save a drowning neighbor have been sued by the victim's family claiming the rescue was inept. Paramedics are frequently dragged into court on charges of negligence. Persons helping accident victims have been forced into costly legal battles. These risks of involvement must be faced. Yet, for the Christian, there is scriptural guidance to help reach a decision on involvement.

In 2 Timothy 1:7, you will find an answer that has helped hundreds of baffled Christians. It reads:

> *For God hath not given us the spirit of* fear, *but of* power, *and of* love, *and of* a sound mind.

Applying the meaning of this promise to involvement produces a Christian plan for action:

1. Have no *fear* of becoming involved.
2. Recognize your *power* to be helpful.
3. Exercise *love* for your neighbor.
4. Seek answers with a *sound mind*.

Involvement will not be impossible if you act reasonably within this framework. Further, these guidelines are more than good psychology. They are based on God's word. What reassurance!

At the first awareness of a neighbor's need, you can do nothing more helpful than to ask the Lord's blessing. More than any other action, prayer dispels fear. Even when the need to act is immediate, a quick prayer to assure yourself of God's presence is priceless. It allows you to act with effectiveness.

A simple illustration may be the best way to visualize a Christian involvement. Imagine you and your neighbor working in adjacent backyards. Your neighbor is using his power mower. All of a sudden he cries out, lets go of the mower, and falls to the ground grasping his foot. Sensing the accident, and need for help, you utter a silent prayer for help and rush over to see what happened:

First, you have *no fear* of becoming involved. Your neighbor has been hurt. There is only one way you can help. It's by becoming involved. Any thoughts about possible legal entanglements vanish. You realize that God has not given you the spirit of fear. You rush over to the neighbor to see how you can help.

Secondly, you recognize your *power* to be helpful. You are the only other person present. It is within your power to see what's wrong, comfort the neighbor, and do whatever else is possible. While God has placed you in this accident scene, he has also promised you the spirit of power. With this spirit, regardless of your abilities, you know you can do some good. This encourages you to examine your neighbor's foot, which has been cut by his lawn mower, and act.

Thirdly, you exercise *love* for your neighbor. Without love in your heart, you might well become angry at your neighbor's carelessness. You might actually hesitate, or worse, refuse to get involved. But God has given you a spirit of love. You loosen your neighbor's shoe, check the cut, take out your handkerchief and apply pressure to control the bleeding. You decide, in love, that you must do all you can to be helpful.

Fourthly, you seek answers with a *sound mind*. Within the limits of your knowledge, God has blessed you with the spirit of a sound mind. You act responsibly. You realize the possible severity of your neighbor's cut foot and get him into the emergency room of the nearest hospital. You help him into your car and drive to the hospital. If it were more serious, you would call for an ambulance.

You go through all four steps of involvement in practically all helping situations. Even in the smallest of love deeds, these four elements come into play. The simple offer of a morning cup of coffee requires the absence of fear in becoming involved; a recognition of your power to make and serve the coffee; an exercise of love toward your neighbor; and the use of a sound mind in concluding that coffee is permissible to serve your neighbor. Rather than shying away from involvement with your neighbors, you probably will end up seeking opportunities. Best of all, the four-step involvement will become automatic in your witnessing.

As you grow in your love deed witness to your neighbors, you will become aware that each must be helped in a particular way. This is perhaps the most compelling reason for a friendly relationship. Only when you become close can you discover real needs, and the special ways to address them. You might think that this is no easy task. You are right. But anything that's worth-while is never easy. This is not as formidable a task as it sounds. You automatically learn need-answers as friendship unfolds. And this should be a joy. With most neighbors, it will not take long before you can "read" them — and know exactly how to act toward them.

As you reach for opportunities to witness, you will notice differences in your responses to certain types of people. One of these types may be the wealthy. You will have to guard against envy in your help toward them. When you find a wealthy neighbor's house, automobile, vacations, or any other possessions, to be superior to yours, the desire to recognize their other needs might weaken. To witness to the rich is similar to selecting a gift for somebody who has everything. Yet there is not a single human being, among all the world's millionaires, who does not have unsolved human needs. The challenge is to find out exactly what they are.

If you are married, you and your spouse can team up to better find hidden needs. Some people, by their very natures, tend to have more perception about people. Others are more perceptive concerning things. A couple, then, can develop a high degree of sensitivity by pooling talents to embrace a wider spectrum of unmet needs. This also applies to selecting the most appropriate love deed. Of course, many needs are deep-seated. You have to dig hard to discover some of the hopes and fears of many people. Sometimes you can discover needs by analyzing a neighbor's words, tone, or inflections. You may also find other clues in facial expressions and body language. Love deeds should answer inaudible cries for help that are squelched by society or pride. This kind of help becomes the strongest heartbeat of an active witness.

Your neighborhood will also impact on what kind of love deeds will be most appreciated. In some areas, there is an "openness" about people in need. There exists a feeling of togetherness that welcomes a helping hand. The affluent suburbs can be a different story. These residents tend to be highly individualistic. They're proud of their self-reliance, and more prone to be cynical about any offer of assistance.

There also exist differing situations in various regions of

our country. At one extreme is the so-called "Bible Belt" where Christian concepts are often broadly embraced. Then, in other states and a number of big cities, such as Chicago, Atlanta, Dallas, and San Francisco, there is varying resistance to Christianity. In New York City, and certain other areas, concentrations of various Jewish, Catholic, Protestant, and other faiths make it imperative to create friendly and tolerant atmospheres. Allowances for deeply ingrained religious heritages must be made. However, love has no quarrel with religions, race, color, sex, or social status. Love recognizes one fundamental truth: we are all children of God. We were told to "go into the whole world," and that you and I will do.

If your neighbors are either quite young or quite elderly, your love deeds demand special tailoring. It is not difficult for us to be shocked at the life-styles of persons at either of these extremes. For instance, a young unmarried couple living together becomes a real challenge for some of us. Or, an older person with attitudes that seem "old fashioned" to us may tax our love. You might find teenagers and pre-teenagers hard to figure. The success of age-group witnessing is in selecting those with whom you feel comfortable. You cannot be all things to all people. God will supply other persons to witness to those whom you find impossible. Never let your failures with certain types of persons discourage you.

Along the way, if you are confronted with an opportunity to witness for those in an age group you do not prefer, you cannot refuse. God has reasons. It would seem intelligent, if at all possible, to concentrate efforts on those with whom you are most compatible. God gave us the power to reason. Use it.

You might find certain ethnic groups the toughest of all to witness to comfortably. Some Christians find this of little hindrance, but I must confess it has been a big problem for me. I stumble and fumble in relating to blacks and Hispanics and pray that this flaw be rooted out of me. God loves us all equally. I cringe when I consciously feel superior, or become condescending. I fight these attitudes, looking forward to my own dream — that day when God changes me and I become ethnically blind. The important thing is to recognize our prejudices, and to seek to treat all people with love and respect.

Like Paul, "that which I do I hate," and when asked to serve ethnic minorities, I follow a course of not ideal, but satisfactory, value. I seek out others who are not troubled with this "thorn in the flesh," and ask them to help. Some Christians are not inhibited in this respect. They can serve wholeheartedly, and give all of themselves to any human being, regardless of ethnicity. If you are one of these people, you are blessed. However, if you have trouble in this regard, seek out others for help with this specialized-audience witnessing. You will find welcome relief from your sense of inadequacy, and, perhaps, help in overcoming it.

Another area of concern is the male/female neighbor problem. There have been no comprehensive studies, to my knowledge, of the relative effectiveness of witnessing to males versus females. You may have no trouble with love deeds toward the opposite gender. If so, you are blessed. But, you probably have noted that some men tend to shy away from witnessing to women. Traditionally, men have been reared to be more reticent in social situations. While women tend to have fewer problems witnessing to either sex. It seems their traditional social training allows more ease in dealing with either sex. If you have these problems, seek out a friend to witness with you. If a problem-witnessing is unavoidable, earnestly pray that, with the Holy Spirit, you can muddle through it. The more attempts you make, the easier it becomes, with the Lord's help.

The educational level of the persons to whom you are witnessing is also a bother to some Christians. Most worry relates to the more highly educated, those in the professions, or of recognized intellectual expertise. To help you face this problem, one concept will be of practical help. Consider that knowledge can be divided into two spheres: facts and feelings. Many of the better educated are long on facts, but short on feelings. This is no mystery considering the typical life of the scholar or professional. To achieve expertise, these persons concentrate on amassing great quantities of facts. Life becomes so occupied with the search, classification, and use of facts that they have time for little else. As a consequence, their lives, many times, become successful but unbalanced.

A life with a shortage of shared feelings creates a vacuum that yearns to be satisfied. What is welcomed by many of these persons is a warm expression of your love and concern. Little acts, like remembering birthdays, extending congratulations for accomplishments, and sending get-well cards, can mean more to the educated than others. Help with the mundane things of life also sparks friendship with the erudite. Your help relating to yard work, recipes, the automobile, entertainment events, or household problems evoke much gratitude. These are "vacuum areas" in the lives of many successful people. As you step forward and help, you are likely to become an extra-special-friend who fills a void in their lives. It is amazing the respect many accomplished persons have for those who show them the meaning of love.

No matter what category into which a neighbor seems to fit, you can witness. You can find that special kind of helpfulness that will open up opportunities to talk about spiritual truths. How wonderful it is to be able to be a practical witness to all your neighbors. Educated or not, rich or poor, male or female, your neighbor mission field is waiting for you.

Because God gives you so many neighbors to care for, can you imagine his not helping? He promises the power of the Holy Spirit. You need never be nervous about your witness. One day you will be given the opportunity to speak out, in answer to questions. Questions, perhaps, about spiritual matters. By this time, your neighbor and you are friends. The neighbor knows and trusts you. There are no barriers to communicating. Your neighbor knows:

1. You are a gentle *being*.
2. You have a gentle *attitude*.
3. You *care* in a gentle way.
4. You give gentle *answers*.

Given this awareness, the Holy Spirit will prepare your neighbor's soul. While you might be nervous about answering questions, you should have no fear. When the questions come from a neighbor, you know that the Holy Spirit is in charge. The same Spirit that puts the questions into the mouth of your neighbor will provide you with the answers. By committing the whole interview into the hands of God, you will have no need to fear. The Scripture states in Matthew 18:20: "For where two or three are gathered together in my name, there am I in the midst of them." You, your neighbor, and the Holy Spirit will visit together. The final outcome will be God's will for your neighbor, you, and His plan.

There is little reason to prepare for the spiritual questions most likely to be asked by neighbors. They are usually ordinary, simple, easy to answer. Nevertheless, the answers can have eternal consequences. Matter-of-fact as they may seem, your answers will make a difference. These you can expect: "Do you attend a church?", "What church?", "Who is your minister?", "Is there a big Sunday school at your church?", "Where is your church located?"

Sad to say, I have never been approached by a neighbor who asked me, "What must I do to be saved?" You probably will be relieved by this probability. The lack of questions dealing directly with salvation should not depress you. Underneath these ordinary questions lies an unspoken desire to talk about spiritual matters. Seldom will the more profound questions be asked. Nor should they be in ordinary contact. How awkward would it be if most conversations insisted on the meaning of God, life, death, or destiny. In the majority of cases, these truths can be better expressed by a minister in a place of worship. To allow this is not to dodge our responsibilities. It is using intelligence to put our unsaved under conditions of maximum spiritual influences.

Does this mean that our witnessing should not be spiritual? If ever the opposite should be practiced, here is the place. Crucial is the respect you give to the Word. Nothing in life is as important as the Word of God. To handle the Word, in a manner that even hints of conceitedness, over-confidence, or casualness is inexcusable. Most laypersons cannot give clarity to the message of salvation. It is enough if you lead your neighbor to sources of authoritative information. The obvious source of guidance is the church. The obvious communicator is the pastoral staff. The obvious job for you and me is to get our neighbor and our church together. This is spiritual witnessing of unselfish excellence.

It is important to fight the egotistical notion that you, personally, are the most powerful force in bringing a neighbor to a saving faith. If you want to be "professional" in the battle for souls, use the whole army of God. Depend on the Holy Spirit as the omnipotent power behind every conversion. Lean on your pastor as the wisest resource you have. Trust that your neighbor can find true love in the fellowship of the congregation. Bring to bear all elements in God's plan for salvation of the human race. Place yourself not first, but last.

It is humbling to realize that nothing will happen except through the grace of the Holy Spirit. Everything you do means little unless the Spirit brings understanding and conviction. Human facts and feelings are barren until they are touched by the Divine. But once the Holy Spirit blesses your witnessing, there are results. Your human efforts become holy and eternal.

Witnessing to your neighbors is simple and easy. Here are seven reasons why a gentle witness to your neighbors fits your more conservative personality:

1. You don't carry the responsibility for a positive outcome. The Holy Spirit does.

2. You don't witness, in a spiritual vein, unless you are first asked spiritual questions.

3. You talk with your neighbor in a climate of established friendship and goodwill.

4. You lean on your pastor, your church, and other lay persons to help.

5. You simply talk, in simple words, about the most familiar subjects — your own faith and experiences.

6. If you can answer your neighbor's questions, great. If you can't, just admit it, and indicate you will find answers. Either way, your neighbor will be most appreciative.

7. You will be filled with joy because, despite your gentleness, you'll know you have skillfully witnessed.

Ideally, your spiritual witness to your neighbor will be confidential conversation. You might be asked, "What do you believe?" The answer should be truthful and humble. I usually state, "Well, I have a childlike faith. I believe in God and in his Son, Jesus, as my Lord and Savior." If the neighbor asks why you have this faith, you can simply state, "Well, the Bible says that's all I have to do to inherit eternal life." If you are led into deeper water, you might further inform your neighbor that you don't know all the answers, but you'll look them up. You have, by answering this way, humbled yourself before your neighbor. You have not flaunted any superior knowledge. You have not confronted or challenged. And, you have stood at your neighbor's side, ready to be of more help.

The further help you can offer finds a number of interesting forms. One of the most appreciated is to offer a copy of the New Testament. Several good versions are available, and I have yet to find a church that will not supply a free copy to help someone become a Christian. There are scores of fine pamphlets, booklets, and books to help those seeking faith.

Supplying literature can become a most effective part of your Christian giving. Literature is greatly prized, not only at the time of the giving, but long afterward. Some Christians have made the distribution of easy-to-understand printed material the central effort in their witness. It has a record of effectiveness.

As your spiritual exchanges with your neighbor expand, you will begin to find it as easy as talking about the weather. Look forward to the realization, by both you and your neighbor, that you really are "about your Father's business." This is a top-of-the-mountain experience that will make you feel like jumping up and singing.

It can come as quite a jolt to discover there exist honest differences. It's hard to face the fact that your interpretation of God's word is not recognized as the truth, the whole truth, and nothing but the truth. It comes as a shock wave, along life's journey, to see one of your cherished beliefs shattered. And, it takes a lot of maturity to respect a neighbor's viewpoint if it is radically different than yours.

The difference in interpretation is in God's hands. You and your neighbor may honestly interpret Scripture differently. Each of you has this right, and each of you can be right. An illuminating reference occurs in John 5:39: "Search the scriptures; for in them ye think ye have eternal life, and they are they which testify of me." God seems to be saying that each of us must work out our personal and particular belief. God did not say, "Listen, all my people, this is the one and only way you must believe to have eternal life . . ." No, he asks that each of us weigh what's in the Scriptures and reach our own conclusions. If God allows for individual interpretations of his word you should also. If your neighbor sees the Scriptures differently than you do, respect these differences. You both may be right. And, someday we will understand why.

If you and your neighbor can't agree, love is the only answer. There is no militant "Onward Christian Soldiers" crushing of the opposing viewpoint. Rather, love dictates a "Softly and Tenderly Jesus Is Calling" approach. It might prove helpful to imagine how Jesus would witness to your dissenting friend. Perhaps you would see your Jesus overflowing with love and compassion. You might imagine him speaking with soft reasonableness. There would be no pressure, no mistaking, no straining to make points. His answers to your neighbor's questions would be softened in love.

You might also presume that Jesus would silently pray for the help of the Holy Spirit. He would ask the Holy Spirit to clear the heart and mind of the neighbor. He would ask that the seed of personal faith become planted in the virgin spiritual soil of yet another soul. Then, with consummate tenderness he might ask, "What think ye of Me?" And, he would be overwhelmed with the response, "My Lord and my God." With tears streaming down his cheeks, Jesus might then say, "Come, neighbor, follow me through this life and eternity. We will be together forever!"

The more you witness to your neighbors, the more you will improve the joy of life. Life is alive when it is being lived for God's purposes. You will look at every neighbor as a gift from God, an opportunity. Your practical love deeds will help you and your neighbors. One after another, they will open their hearts and minds to you. They will come to value you. As friendships develop, more questions will be answered with gentleness and love. This is the gentle witness that works.

This type of witnessing can give you a joy-filled life. It can provide a vision of a someday, when you are in God's house, looking at many friends and saying, "Hi, Neighbor!"

Chapter 5

It's True — Church Members Need Help

If your reaction toward witnessing to church members is, "You must be kidding!" you're not too different from millions of others. The idea seems ridiculous. Aren't church members already Christians? Aren't church members active and committed? The answer is yes — and no! Perhaps you have doubts about the necessity of witnessing within the church. Consider the following three items appearing in the Sunday edition of a large metropolitan newspaper:

The first is from one of the most popular comic strips, "Hagar The Horrible," and featured two men with placards reading, "The End is Near," and "Love Thy Neighbor." The men were hitting each other over the head with their posters. They were having a real brawl. Hagar quips to a friend, "Probably a religious argument!"

The second item began with a dominant headline screaming: "Churchwoman Is Charged In Choir Slaying." After dwelling on all the sordid details, the story concluded with, "The Rev. Salomar Smith, pastor of the church, stated, 'They were both long-time members of the church. Both of them are fine ladies!' "

The third item involved the religion page's coverage of the famed "Hour of Power" television program of the Rev. Robert Schuller. Highlighted was the singing idol of millions, B. J. Thomas. His featured song was:

Love is our common ground,
Love has no limits,
Love has no bounds,
Love is our common ground!

These three totally different concepts of Christianity must tear at your heart. If you can live with this, you are fortunate.

But, what about the millions of unchurched? Exposed to these saint/sinner images of Christians, they might well think, "What a bunch of hypocrites!"

We realize we are sinners saved by grace, but few non-Christians can put this thought together in proper perspective. In fact, many of us have trouble with this saint/sinner complex. Worst of all, the media love this type of story — the saints who strayed! And, the public seems to eat it up. Are you thinking, "Why does this happen? How do these events get started? What can I do to help?" These questions are the reasons church members need your witness.

How you can bring the witnessing elements of *being, attitude, caring,* and *answers* to bear on fellow church members? It requires a "sound mind." To be intelligent about your "in-house" witness requires a knowledge of your fellow member. Just because persons are members, you cannot fit them into a mold. There are many kinds of Pentecostals, Presbyterians, Catholics — you name it. Church denomination is but a minor clue to personal beliefs and behavior. Every individual member is unique, and is influenced by a variety of factors including gender, physique, personality, occupation, education, heritage, health, family, money, denomination, and charisma.

Understanding these uniquenesses will give you a double-barrelled advantage:

First Barrel — You have the information necessary to make an effective, selective approach.

Second Barrel — You can better understand where the person is coming from, the "why" of the questions asked. Paralleling the eleven unique characteristics mentioned, consider these suggestions for handling them:

1. *Female versus Male Members* — This obvious distinction is quite often overlooked. Women and men have been traditionally trained to respond somewhat differently to social and spiritual contact. You probably recognize that women

are often more comfortable with social skills. In your witness to them, consider that they may appreciate a showing of love, an emphasis on compassion, a recognition of the sensible. Male members are often not as well tuned-in to social complexities. They may have more interest in abstract ideas, preferring the tangible. However, let your own experience with each individual dictate how you handle individual situations. To simply recognize individual differences is constructive.

2. *The "Physical Member"* — The bodily characteristics of a member are important to your witness. Observation tends to suggest that different physiques require special approaches. Unfortunately, our society holds some rather strictly defined attitudes toward physical appearance and body type. Magazines, television, and storefronts promote these ideal stereotypes every day. As gentle witnesses, we need to be sensitive to the insecurities which they often create. Adjust, if you can, to any "undesirable" physical uniquenesses of fellow church members.

3. *The "Personality" Member* — Easily recognizable, in any church, are the excessively "outgoing" members. These personalities cannot help themselves. They seem born to be aggressive, loud, and domineering. While it may be difficult, let your witness to them be as aggressive as possible. Many times they will be surprised and influenced. You can best relate by attempting a loudness level similar to theirs. If their loudness is merely an act of compensation, they will often tone down. You can then proceed to communicate on a more normal level. Otherwise, difficult as it is to a more gentle personality, "answer in kind."

4. *Professional Members* — Many occupations are represented in the average congregation — blue collar, white collar, specialists, and professionals. You might be restrained in your witness to professionals out of respect. Remember, God deals identically with all mankind, whether they are

production line sinners, or professional sinners. All equally need his salvation. Likewise, all need the love of your witness. The Holy Spirit humbles the elevated, and elevates the humble. Your witness, with his help, transcends all occupational differences. Doctor, lawyer, beggarman, thief — give your love equally.

5. *Educated Members* — A factor that unduly inhibits some Christians is unequal education. Yet, it is not uncommon for testimony from an elementary school graduate to profoundly influence the life of a Ph. D. The reason for this type of witnessing impact is the difference between worldly knowledge and spiritual experience — between familiarity with facts and experience with feelings. Your *being — attitude — caring — answers* can rise above all educational degrees. You need never fear loving the highly educated — they'll love back like we all do.

6. *"Status" Members* — There may be members of your congregation who never miss an opportunity to remind you of their illustrious ancestors. Some may constantly brag about their immediate family. Heritage and family may make a difference, but not an important difference. These are proud members, and the Lord does not have many words of encouragement for them. You should try to overlook references to superior lineage. Don't "put them down," but neither be impressed. Remember, we all have the identically same heritage as Christians — we are children of God and joint heirs with Christ. How "royal" can we all be!

7. *Sick Members* — If you enjoy good health, it may be difficult to understand the attitudes of the sick. Chronic illness, whether cough or cancer, affects the whole mental and spiritual outlook. Constant pain, anguish, and anxiety can lead to depression. When you are with a sick member, make allowances. These members afford you wonderful opportunities for caring and sharing. Their needs are many. You can help make their lives more bearable until "God shall wipe away all the tears from their eyes."

8. *"Family" Members* — Younger married couples, with several children, will have certain program preferences. Children's and youth programs are vital to these people. Conversely, the singles, and many older members, live alone. Their interests are understandably different. Seek out these familial facts and let them become the key to unlocking doors of better understanding. Addressing the family unit correctly, in your caring and concern, can make all the difference. Love and understanding can be trusted guides.

9. *Rich and Poor Members* — Cleric and laity too often give special treatment to members at the extreme economic levels. How human it is to pander to the rich member, or to discount the poor. What is wrong is our definition of "riches." The real riches we all have, as Christians, are in Christ. You are a "joint heir" of the "unsearchable riches of Christ!" Would you barter this for a million dollars? One trillion dollars? More? You simply should not be influenced by material riches or poverty — treat all alike. Let your love flow over both wealth and poverty.

10. *Sectarian Members* — All church members have some degree of denominational bias. If it weren't so, there would be but one denomination in our country. How wonderful it is to have freedom of religion — the liberty to select the church of our choice. Among your own membership, as in most churches, you may find those who attach extreme importance to certain beliefs, creeds, or sacraments. So sincere are these members that they lack appreciation and respect for all other viewpoints. In talking to these church members, express just one viewpoint — Christ, and him alone. If asked questions about denominational specifics, you can rely on the metaphor of the human body: the head, arms, legs, etc., are all different, yet all necessary for a whole body. This witness will speak strongly to "sectarian" church members.

11. *Charismatic Members* — Some church members may be given special gifts — evangelism, healing, speaking in tongues, music. Whatever the spiritual gift, be glad for it. Your

attitude must be one of respect, even though you may not agree. Give whatever loving, caring, and sharing you can.

12. *Passive Members* — By far, the great majority of church members to whom you will witness are passive. Yet, they must be important because God has made so many of them. Non-charismatic, non-demonstrative, numerically in the majority, these members are "children" of God. They have a simple, child-like faith which they do not express, but which must be acceptable to our Lord. Did he not say, "Suffer little children, and forbid them not to come unto Me; for of such is the Kingdom of Heaven." Let's do it.

This listing is quite incomplete. Understanding the particular personality of the church member is important. Only then can you tailor — most perfectly — your attitudes and actions. These differences among the members are not weaknesses, but strengths. Christian individuality, and the many resulting church denominations, broaden the acceptability of the Christian church. You, and I, can realize that though there are hundreds of denominations, there exists one unity — Christ.

The Rt. Reverend Richard S. Emrich put it in the proverbial nutshell:

> *Every Christian is baptized into Christ, with no mention of a particular denomination; and since all have been grafted into Christ, all are one in Him. And, our brotherhood in Him reveals the spirit with which men everywhere should be approached, whether they are Christians or not. He is the Saviour of the world and the Restorer of human unity.*

Even secular teachers have a good grasp on the importance of Christian unity. Here are the wise words of Frank Crane: "Jesus was the only teacher tall enough to see over the fences that divide the human race into compartments."

No matter into which compartment your fellow church members fit, your concern for them can be one of uplift and praise. There does not exist a single Christian who cannot be helped by honest praise. When we fulfill our faith by praising

God's people, we are praising Him. He desires this of us, not strictly for his own pleasure, but for the joy it can bring to ourselves. The words of William Law are right to the point:

> *If anyone would tell you the shortest, surest way to happiness and perfection, he must tell you to make it a rule to yourself to thank and praise God for everything that happens to you. For it is certain that whatever seeming calamity happens to you, if you thank and praise God for it, you turn it into a blessing.*

If God approves of praise to him — for both good and bad — the example should find acceptance when used to help our fellow man. As a part of your witness to church members, it soon becomes a habit to praise those around you. The kind words, loving actions, and caring attitudes of any church member can be praised doubly. First, to the person, and second, to others. This results in "Praise Power." Others pick up the practice. Soon a whole congregation develops a praising attitude. It is very hard to imagine just how much praise helps people.

If you have trouble finding something to praise about a fellow-member, you are not an exception. It takes awareness and practice. You can find hundreds of opportunities to lift up people before God and man. As a starting point in developing your own "Praise Power," check this list:

1. *Smile.* Yes, just a simple smile aimed at a particular person can be meaningful. This is a non-verbal, non-contact act. Often overlooked, the smile implies worlds of praise. And, you can do it; anybody can do it. So, smile, Christian, smile! It's easy, it's lovely, it's contagious.

2. *Smile and Nod.* When you smile, a nod in the proper direction will emphasize the exclusiveness of your attention. Don't over-emphasize the nod, it is not necessary. But that slight downward action of the head really personalizes your smiling praise.

3. *Shake Hands*. The warmth of a handshake provides another outlet. Long understood in secular life, in a church atmosphere, the handshake has deeper meaning. A firm, but not muscular, handshake says, "I'm on your side and we're both on God's side!"

4. *Recognize By Name*. Is there a soul who does not like to be addressed by name. Why? Well, it's a totally exclusive recognition. It's easy for some to do, hard for those with more ordinary memories. As much as you can — put the right name on the right face — and give praise through identification.

5. *Use the Word "Good."* Whether it's "Good morning!", "Have a good day!", or "It's good to see you!" the inclusion of the word "good" gives uplift. Even if it's a bad day, use of the word "good" brightens the conversation. Make sure you include a "good" in your praise. Don't you think it's a "good" idea?

6. *The Hug*. While widely used as a sign of Christian love, the hug should be dealt with cautiously. In some parts of the country, and in certain denominations, hugging is expected. Not all church members, however, find public hugging to their liking. Practiced with discretion, it is hard to find a finer expression of Christian agape.

7. *The Joyous Occasion*. Praise is automatic when a fellow member is experiencing great joy. Whatever the reason — a new child, a wedding, a conversion — special appreciation and affection is in order. Even the more sedate Christian can give vent to feelings with a shaking of hands, slapping on the back, hugs and kisses. And, don't forget to praise the Lord, also, for the occasion.

8. *The Sorrowful Occasion*. This is where praise to our God and our fellow worshiper is the hardest to give. If you find the ability to do it properly, you will share in a great experience. You will never be forgotten for your act and words. Particularly at the death of a loved one, your careful praise can be of supreme support.

9. *Correspondence.* Some persons cannot express emotion verbally, but are absolute masters at putting it in writing. There's always special enjoyment in receiving a letter, memo, or greeting. In times of important celebration or bereavement, nothing can substitute for the written word. Praising by writing also has a lasting quality and can be savored many times. Do it — do it as often as you can.

10. *The Greeting Card.* This is their age! And, it's really fun finding a card with the right kind of message for the occasion. Cards are not only great messengers, they are the easiest "bringers of joy." Beside your signature, when you send a card, remember to write a personal line or two. What joy personalized greeting cards can bring. And, if you find them too expensive, draw one of your own. You'd be surprised how much this is appreciated.

11. *After The Sermon.* An ideal time to praise a fellow member. Everybody is ready to socialize, in fact, perhaps even encouraged by the pastor. If you don't know the parishioners, praise the way they look, sing, or participate. If you're acquainted, make sure you praise positively. Pick out something good about the sermon, the church, or the person you're talking to. Praise sometimes becomes "the tie that binds."

12. *Praise the Officers.* The hours most church officers put in on their work could set many a Guinness record. Even a small word of appreciation here is terrifically encouraging. Many church members criticize their officers . . . few praise them. When you praise your officers for the work they're doing, everybody in the church will benefit.

13. *Don't Forget The Ushers.* Members really appreciate the cheerful attitudes and seating skills of good ushers. Yet, few praise them, either to their face, or to other members. Don't you wonder why? Your sincere comments about the ushers will help your worship service. It's a little praise that brings big benefits.

14. *The Music.* More often than not, church music is taken

for granted. The organist, the choir members, the soloists —
all work like beavers. Your recognition of their work is the
least you can do for them. Think about the meaning of the
music. Think about the beauty with which it is brought to the
congregation. Be specific in your praise of the songs and the
musicians.

15. *Young Members.* Can you remember back when you
were a youngster? Some adult church member may have paid
attention to you? Even a short, "Hello there — you look nice
this morning!" was remembered a good long time. Or, "Hi,
Pat, how's the baseball team doing?" was the kind of attention that meant a lot. As the years rush by, these youngsters
soon become the church membership and officers. Yes, a
youngster's exuberance can be distracting, but put a little of
your Christian "praise power" to work on them. If they see
Christ in you, they'll put more of him in their own lives.

16. *The Neglected.* Sadly, every church has its neglected
members. They're the chronically ill, the elderly, the hangers-
on of life. Many of them have made significant past contri-
butions to the progress of the church. People forget so fast.
Search your memory, or ask friends about them. A word of
remembrance, perhaps a little note or card, can mean much.
These little communications can bring encouragement to their
rather lonely lives. What a worthwhile witness!

Don't confine your church member "praise power" to this
list of opportunities. As your sensitivity develops, new opportunities will jump out at you. Grab them. As you give praise
and encouragement, your church will take on a new glow.
Don't be surprised if visitors comment on how friendly your
church is. Don't be startled, either, if your personal spiritual
life takes on new zest. If you ever question the value of praising fellow church members (and others, too) re-read that golden
verse; Philippians 4:8:

Finally, brethren, whatsoever things are true, whatsoever things are honest, whatsoever things are just, whatsoever things are pure, whatsoever things are of good report; if there be any virtue, and if there be any praise, think on these things.

Think on these things and give praise to your fellow church members. You'll truly glorify God.

Chapter 6

Easy As Whistling While You Work

You and I are challenged daily to witness to our fellow-workers. Many are in desperate need of help, but won't admit it. Previously, you might not have touched this type of witnessing with a ten-foot pole. But, by now, some of your fears have vanished. Following will be step-by-step explanations of "how to do it." Worker witness can be easy, and effective. Let's examine one true-life experience:

A young reporter for a Chicago newspaper was ordered into his editor's office. The editor was terse, "Find out why John Smith, President of Land Steel, received the 'Communicator of the Year Award' from the United Nations. Get going!"

It was like interviewing a king. The office of Mr. Smith was designed to impress. Across a good five feet of polished mahogany desk, Mr. Smith posed an interviewing challenge. Yet, as the steel tycoon held out his hand, the pressure seemed to lessen. His eyes, his voice, his manner, all resulted in an attitude of, "How can I help you, son?"

His answers to the reporter's questions were precise but kindly. He gave as much information as possible. He even suggested new avenues of inquiry. The interview became a joy.

As the questioning was coming to a close, the reporter noticed something. A six-inch high ivory cross, mounted on a heavy silver base, was on the desk, directly in front of Mr. Smith. The reporter felt impelled to ask, "I can't help but be attracted by that cross, Mr. Smith. Is it special to you?"

The wise Mr. Smith offered, "Whatever small measure of success I've achieved as a communicator I owe to that cross. And, to the person who sent it to me. He was a missionary in Africa who became a good friend. He was one of the finest

Christians I've ever known. Here, take it and read what's inscribed on the bottom of the base.''

The reporter read the etched message:

To my good friend, John Smith. May the precious words below come to mean as much to you as they mean to me.

"But as He which hath called you is holy, so be you holy in all manner of conversation."

1 Peter 1:15

In discovering President Smith's secret of success, that young newspaperman learned a priceless principle. It was to guide him for the rest of his life. It was to steer him to the religion editorship of one of America's largest newspapers. It helped him write more than a hundred *Reader's Digest* stories. It made possible the writing of a four-star, inspirational movie. This unusual witness by President Smith, in the course of business, truly magnified Christ!

You might say, however, ''That's a wonderful story about an influential man, but I'm just an ordinary employee. I'm sure I couldn't do anything so effective.'' Well, ''it ain't necessarily so!'' For more years than I can rightly remember, I used a similar technique. It is a method that any employee can use successfully. See if you can't work out a way to follow this method in your own working situation; here's what I did:

For many years, I made it a habit to read my Bible every day. Sometimes, extensively; in the busiest times, perhaps only a verse or two. To make it as convenient as possible, I decided to get an extra Bible and put it on top of my desk at work. Usually, I did my reading when I first arrived in the morning.

As a gentle witness, however, it was the physical presence of the Bible that did the trick. Fellow workers, sales persons, or acquaintances, who came in to talk with me, really couldn't help noticing the desk-top Bible. This, I now feel, was a major catalyst in generating spiritual conversations . . . the type of talk that might otherwise never occur.

I wouldn't have to say a word. It usually happened something like this: The other person would open up with a remark such as "I see you have your Bible on your desk; do you ever get to read it?" It didn't matter how this initial inquiry was put. Nearly always it became an opportunity to "get into" talk about the book, the church, and faith. This became a way to witness that has resulted in conversions and commitments.

There are other work-area objects that will start spiritual conversations.

Small statuettes, crosses of unusual materials, symbolic artifacts, and carved or printed slogan panels. Some Christians I have known put photographs to use. Snapshots of their church, a gathering, or a retreat group — all help start a conversation. Important is the fact that your witness is not aggressive. The initiative comes from the other person. From there on in, all you have to do is to have a pleasant conversation.

If done in good taste, it is helpful to have a Christian publication handy. It can be very inexpensive. Many churches have a variety of periodicals, booklets, even New Testaments which they will supply you. Try to get literature that has a tie-in to your place of work. Or, to a common work problem. Be selective about giving out this type of literature. Make sure it doesn't appear this is something you do for everyone. Don't broadcast literature willy-nilly. Look for a piece that has specific application to the persons involved.

You might feel that everyone in your place of work would benefit by reading a certain printed piece. While this may be true, the widespread distribution of literature can be counterproductive. The working atmosphere is one of a team. To ignore this fact, and flood fellow workers with Christian literature indicates an attitude that might be unforgiven. It displays a lack of compassion for the individual problems of your close fellow workers. If you really love them, you will go to the trouble of being patient with each of them — discovering each individual's peculiar circumstances — and only then selecting an appropriate piece of literature.

Most work places have rules about promoting any specific religion on their premises. This makes sense. If some policy were not established, serious religious discriminations could develop. Friends might become enemies. Promotions and "perks" might be given on the basis of beliefs. Workers might become guilty of not giving the job its proper attention. There are exceptions, of course. Some Christian-owned businesses have the blessing of its owners for employees to promote the faith. If you are fortunate enough to work for such an organization, count your blessings. However, in these Christian organizations, by their very structure, the opportunity to witness to the unsaved or unchurched is greatly diminished.

An effective part of your witness is the attitude you have about your work. Fellow workers are not dumb; they'll surmise that you are a Christian. They'll keep a sharp eye on you to see whether or not you are living up to your beliefs. Your witness is not easy. You must set an example. Your work must be "tops." Your attitudes toward your fellow workers and the company must be beyond criticism. Believe me, this is difficult; you might think impossible. Yet, it is precisely here where you can excel.

You are asked to be true to God, and true to self. You are also asked to be true to your job, and true to your fellow workers. You can exhibit these truths and be admired for them. This Christian honesty is not without its dangers. If you consistently stand for what is just and right, you might become unpopular. There are instances where such a stand may cost you your job. Even your reputation. Consider just a few situations:

Case A: You are a production line worker. A rate has been set for your line which you feel is justifiable. Your union, in their strategy, urges your production line to slow down until certain demands are met. You have a dual loyalty, yet you feel that one of the alternatives is right, the other wrong. How should you act?

Case B: You are a secretary to a social service executive. The executive has been spending increasingly large amounts of time away from the job on personal business. As a result, the effectiveness of your office is decreasing. You like your boss, but you feel what is happening is inexcusable. One day, a headquarters' investigator visits, and privately asks you what you think is wrong. How do you answer?

Case C: You are the marketing director of a high technology company manufacturing electronic parts. You are invited to an informal dinner given by two of your competitors. At the dinner, a strong suggestion is made that the prices of certain parts by "stabilized" at an illegal identical price by all three manufacturers. This, you are told, would eliminate "disruptive" price wars. How do you react?

While each of these problems calls for the wisdom of a Solomon, they are not unusual. The moral atmosphere in which many Christians work is often far from ideal. If you "give in" to satisfy fellow workers, or your boss, what happens to your Christian example? It is unfair to be asked to compromise your Christian convictions just to provide financial benefits. By "going along," you open yourself up to criticisms of being "hypocritical." The real answers lie deep within your soul, and will come forth only after prayer. This is not a "cop out." Prayer is the most necessary step you can take.

You might have heard simplistic solutions to questions of this character. They insist the right thing to do is obvious — so do it! Would that it were that easy. Our jobs are vital to the survival of ourselves and our families. To put our job in jeopardy is a serious matter. Does God ask Christians to endanger the welfare of themselves, their spouses, and even their children — in order to set a Christian example in the work place? Perhaps yes! It could be a means of testing faith. It could be a chastening. It certainly could be a check-up on the quality of your witness. Yet, as simple humans, we wonder if it is necessary. God could change the circumstances at the work place and eliminate the problem. Why doesn't he?

If God allows problems to exist, what are your options? The first is to be a Christian hero, stand up to your boss or fellow worker and say either, "This is wrong," or, "You are wrong," or, "I'll have no part of it!" So, what is likely to happen then? If you are allowed to stay at work, you have now made a number of enemies who will either tend to ignore or fight you. Or, if the issue is serious enough, you are frozen in a no-future job. Worse, you are asked to leave. Happily, if you stand up for what's right, your fellow workers might see your way of thinking. You, then, come out of the dilemma with a powerful witness.

Many of these thorny ethical issues in the work area are open to compromises and diplomacy. Seldom is any issue all black or all white. There is always the "other side of the story." You face the problem, as a Christian, of being "in the world," but not, "of the world." It is this ambivalence that causes problems. But, it also provides solutions. Many times it is possible to convey to fellow workers that, while you see their point, you can't fully support them on moral grounds. This approach is less dogmatic. It indicates you have considered their side of the problem. However, it does not conform to your religious beliefs. You can make your opposition known while leaving the door open for further discussion.

Our Lord provides for differences of opinion and interpretation. There are sincere Christians on both sides of the abortion question. There are sincere Christians on both sides of the nuclear bomb issue. There are sincere Christians on both sides of the school prayer issue. You have chosen your stand on these issues, but you cannot, in conscience, condemn other Christians who disagree with you. Why? Because God loves them and influences them as much as he does you. It is on the stone wall of imponderables that we keep banging our heads. Someday, we will know all the right answers. Someday, we will live together in perfect love. Right now, we see the answers dimly, if we see them at all. But, should we not try to live in love? Regardless!

Properly handling ethical problems in the work place takes patience, intelligence, and experience. The more skilled you become in this area, the more respect you'll earn. As fellow workers accept you and your views, they will trust you to a greater degree. Nevertheless, in the work place, what you do is more important than what you say. How you do your job, how you dress, how you participate in activities, all have major effects on your witness opportunities.

For most Christians, doing their jobs well is a built-in trait. Within you is a concept of fairness which demands that you honestly earn your wages. When you give your best, when you work your hardest, when you reflect a positive work attitude — you please yourself and your associates. At work, you should set a Christian work example. You cannot effectively stand up for work-ethics if your personal work-effort is lacking. As they say, "It doesn't wash." You don't have to be the best worker, but you can be the best worker you are capable of being. This is example. It is bound to attract other workers to your Christian way of living.

Organizations realize, however, that all work, and no play, make Jack and Jill unproductive employees. So, they have outside activities — most times well scheduled and administered. Other activities are organized by employees themselves. Events may include picnics, golf, tennis, bowling, softball, touch football, volleyball, parties, and special events at Christmas or other holidays. This spectrum of outside activities presents a different challenge to the Christian trying to set a good example.

Being outside the organization, the restraints of the work place can be carelessly observed. How do you act in these activities, to protect the quality of your witness?

Your participation will be watched. Some, who might characterize you as being "goody-goody," will be looking to further put down your attitudes. Don't give them this opportunity. First, make up your mind to eliminate activities that are on the fringes of acceptability. There might be a hunting weekend where the main activity is drinking, or, poker parties where gambling persists. Avoid such wholesome activity as bowling, if the emphasis is placed on alcohol consumption. But, you should avoid being negative — and this is not too difficult. Simply select one or two of the activities that are constructive, and jump in with both feet. Volunteer to be on the committee for the event, go the extra mile, show fellow workers that you're "with them." If the activity is "right" — go for it!

Select the one, or more, wholesome activity that appeals to you and become active. If you are not proficient in any of them, join the one that you like the most, and work at it. The better you are at any pastime, the more you'll enjoy it. Even if none appeal to you, for whatever reason, force yourself into it. Work on it like you would any other hard problem. If you show progress, you'll win admiration from your fellow workers. No one will expect you to be active in everything. But, if you make even one activity "your thing," your fellow workers will be more understanding. If you become really good in a certain sport or skill, you will win admiration. It's worth the effort to excel. It will make you a more effective witness in your workplacc.

Sometimes you have to "grab the bull by the horns" to insure wholesome recreational projects. Where good programs are lacking, organize some of your own. First, make sure to get permission from your superiors. In one instance, Christian workers organized an all-season musical program. They selected certain local cultural programs, obtained favorable group prices, and made it a huge success. Another group organized a large number of employees and practically took over a local roller skating rink for their own fun. A third business group worked out an evening of swimming fun at a local indoor pool. All these activities were held in wholesome atmospheres and posed genuine competition to questionable activities. Once Christians "roll up their sleeves" on any program, it is difficult to find fault.

Another area the Christian can endorse is membership in a business, social, or civic organization. Activity is applauded in such fellowships as the P.E.O. Sisterhood, American Business Women's Association, the American Red Cross, Women's Club, Chamber of Commerce, Rotarians, Kiwanis, and other similar groups. Programs of these groups obtain publicity and, if you hold office, you're bound to get media exposure. As your reputation for this type of achievement becomes known, it can be helpful. The Christian purpose of establishing this kind of an image is not an ego trip. It is to prove that you are not a "narrow-minded" person to the unsaved or unchurched among your working friends. In this sense, you broaden your interests in the interest of the Lord.

There are several youth-oriented organizations that can help enhance you in the eyes of your "macho type" fellow employees. One group works, in a general way, for Christ on college campuses. The other promotes Christianity among athletes — collegiate and professional. In our youth-oriented, muscle-inclined society, association with these groups is helpful. It breaks down old wives' tales about Christians being less than vital human beings. When you show interest in these groups, talk about them, and encourage them, you build a strong Christian presence. Sports-minded workers are likely to know the Christian viewpoints expressed by leading coaches and players. They probably are aware that prayer groups are held before competition. They've listened to statements of faith from

Olympic medal winners. Your interest in these spiritually-acclimated athletes cannot help but boost your acceptance among workers.

It is not necessary to be an active participant in sports to gain notice. You can be an informed, interested spectator. A close friend is an avid baseball and tennis fan. She watches television, listens to radio, and attends competitions whenever she can. Most interestingly, she has a whole group of acquaintances who admire her for her knowledge. She knows the players, the records, and schedules, and is a fascinating conversationalist even with people who know little about the games. Imagine what a background like this would mean in making friends with fellow workers. Whether you are male or female, a spectator knowledge of sports will give you "common ground" with the most macho workers in your organization. In case there is any question, my friend is a Christian with a truly unusual witness.

Setting yourself into an "accepted" position through the various ways outlined has but one major goal. It is to make you more effective. As your attitudes and actions in the work place open doors of friendship, it becomes easy as "falling off a log" to care and share. As employees become friends, their spiritual needs become clearer. They will realize that you just might be the one to take into their confidence. When this happens, you will uncover ways to care for them, to share with them, to love them with Christian concern. You already know the strongest witness is one of deeds. The tangible help you are able to give will be your success. As love cannot fail — neither can you.

It's all worthwhile when your fellow workers begin to ask spiritual questions. They know you are concerned about them. Once they accept you, they will open up and seek your opinions. And it all happens without one iota of "aggressive" action. This development of opportunities is worth all the patience and time it takes. You'll know that when they take your witness seriously.

Fellow workers are a priceless personal missionary field. Think of the scope if every Christian could have a solid witness to those who work with them. This is the goal of the gentle witness in your work place. Become a worker who inspires others in their jobs. Be a worker who might well interest others in the "Boss" of it all.

Chapter 7

The Sick Are Something Else!

There are people who never visit the sick. They flat-out say they can't do it. You wonder why. Most of us, at our worst, feel a special kind of helplessness when visiting the sick. It might have something to do with the sights, sounds, and smell of the hospital. You know that, if you were ill, you'd like a visitor. But exactly how to become a good visitor, yourself, is something else. You want to bring a good size dose of hope, cheer, and comfort. Somehow, this looms as a nearly impossible task. Your witness to the ill, nevertheless, can be accomplished. Before looking into a remarkably workable plan, let's examine some background.

Before you make any hospital visit, take a good look at your motives. Has it ever occurred to you that it's just possible your visit to a sick friend is self-serving? It might be looked upon as a duty and used for selfish reasons. The rationale behind this not-too-unusual behavior could be one of several:

1. It is a required act, demanded by good breeding — it's good for your ego.

2. It is a matter of reciprocity — your visit will insure being visited when you are ill.

3. It reflects favorably on you among mutual friends — boosts your self esteem.

4. It provides you with an up-to-the-minute lively report to bring back to all your mutual friends.

You may feel this is being too cynical. Yet in a lifetime of sick room and hospital visits, it has been nigh impossible not to suspect motives. All of us have, at one time or another, been painfully aware of the obvious. As a Christian, and specifically as a witness, you certainly should examine yourself.

Ask for pure motives when approaching hospital visitations. The main reasons for visiting is to show love and help heal. What the visit will mean to you, and your friends, is secondary, if that. Like the good Samaritan, to be truly loving, you must focus on improving the physical condition of your sick friend.

If only one person at a time can visit — respect the policy. If the rules state that you cannot stay longer than ten minutes, don't stay eleven. If you are told not to do anything that might excite the patient, make sure you don't. Most certainly, don't look alarmed when you first come bedside and notice the technological maze of tubes, bottles, wires, and electrodes. These are outward indications of modern treatment. They are to be appreciated, rather than deplored. Be happy it's there, put on a smile, know that all the equipment is working to speed recovery.

Your attitude toward the sick person should mirror your faith. Knowing that nothing can separate you, and the patient, from the love of God in Christ is reason to be encouraging. Before you visit, prayer can help. Before you get out of your car, in the hospital parking lot, a short prayer is in order. Ask for the right attitude, the right words, and the right thoughts. Continue in prayer as you move on to the hospital room. When you first see the patient, let encouragement and hope shine from your face. You have been appointed as an ambassador of Christ, to help the sick. Appreciate the opportunity. Forget self, focus on the patient, and praise God in your heart.

The hospital room, itself, can be one of the most beautiful sanctuaries in the world. No stained glass windows, no soaring ceilings, no soul-comforting music, to be sure. Yet there is a certain atmosphere which galvanizes. It separates the trivial from the truth. It brings an awareness of the value of life. It is a place where God is at work — where the Holy Spirit is present, eager to comfort and heal the soul. It is the place where multitudes have committed their lives to Christ. Truly, the hospital room is a sanctuary for body and soul.

As you enter this room, realize that the patient has done some recent thinking about life. The illness need not be life-threatening to spark this reaction. The transition from health to illness comes as a shock. Egos collapse under the strain. The pride of life is transformed into a grasp for life. The patient's wealth, reputation, and importance take on second-rate consideration. They are replaced by a dependency on doctors, nurses, and, yes, God. This is the patient whom you are coming to visit. To comfort. To encourage. To help.

How much you can do, on any one visit, depends in great measure on the condition of the patient. Obviously, if heavily sedated, or in a coma, patients cannot communicate. Some unconscious patients are aware of what is being said, even though they cannot respond. Be careful of all your words at the bedside. Be optimistic, encouraging, never negative even as you talk to the doctor, nurses, or other visitors. Converse as if you knew the patient understood your every word or reaction. Show no shock at the sight of bandaging, drainage, or hospital hardware. This is not always easy, but imagine how appreciative the patient will be. It's a tall order for you, but remember, you are God's witness. Be brave in your caring.

Sit close to the side of the bed. The patient, even if "out of it," will probably sense your presence. Through the third person, the Holy Spirit, yours is not a spirit of fear — but of power, of love, and of a sound mind. With his help, you can have confidence that you can witness in spite of everything. Many patients, only partially conscious, have startling visions or experiences they might share with you. If they do, treat them as real communications. Visions of heaven, of the deceased, or of other spiritual experiences are common. Some patients have visions of Christ. These phenomena should not be discounted. Rather, put the best possible construction on the whole concept. Accept them. Assure the patient that God is with him or her, and showing his loving concern in this manner. This alone can be a wonderful witness.

Among most doctors, there is the recognition that God helps heal. Nurses share these same beliefs. The idea that doctors rely solely on medical science to heal has long since passed. It is not uncommon for doctors, before surgery, to pray for help and guidance. You would be hard pressed to find any doctor who would scoff at the part religious belief takes in the healing process. In recent years, prominent specialists have testified to this belief in nationwide print media and television. As sophistication in health care reaches mind-boggling complexity, dependence on God to provide total healing has increased. If you talk about God's healing with the patient, you can be almost certain that the doctor will approve.

God and the doctor are quite a partnership. Each needs the other. As a Christian, you recognize the importance of God in the healing process. You should also appreciate the value of the doctor and medical science. Those well-meaning sects that refuse medical care can find themselves, and their believers, in serious trouble. In sick visitation, if you have any knowledge of the quality of the doctor, the nurses, or the hospital, emphasize it. Let the patient know that the resources of science, and the love of God, are working together to heal.

Bringing Hope to the Patient

You can find strength in the fact that there are many scriptural references to "hope." For the sick, one of the most helpful is Psalm 43:5:

> *Why art thou cast down, O my soul? and why art thou disquieted within me? Hope in God: for I shall yet praise him, who is the health of my countenance, and my God.*

You may want to quote this, or simply suggest it as a reading when you've left. It can be a spiritual transfusion with miraculous potency.

Other verses you can use are:

"And the prayer of faith shall save the sick." (James 5:15)

"Let us therefore come boldly unto the throne of grace, that we may obtain mercy, and find grace to help in time of need." (Hebrews 4:16)

"Nothing can separate us from the love of God which is in Christ Jesus." (Romans 8:37-39)

If you cannot memorize, or are embarrassed to quote Scripture, don't let that stop you. Pick out a good verse, and write it down on a small file card. When you visit the patient, it's easy to say you just ran across this verse and thought it might be appreciated. You can read it out loud. Or, simply leave it with the patient.

It would probably be surprising to learn how many times the patient will pick up the card and read it. If you like this idea, plan to leave a personally written "Bible verse card" on every visit. These verses will instill hope. They can give comfort. And, it's so easy a way to witness. Even if they're not referred to often, the patient will appreciate the thought behind them.

Upon entering the sickroom, your first hope-filled expression should be a smile. Smile, regardless of any discouraging change in appearance of the patient. Smile even though there is an array of threatening apparatus. Smile to radiate hope. "How can I do that," you might ask, "if the outlook is bad?" You can sincerely smile because Paul said, in Romans 8, that nothing — absolutely nothing — can separate the patient from the love of God in Christ Jesus. That initial smile is not a "paste-on." It's the real thing. This sincerity will not go undetected by the patient. Your smile at the bedside will be a signal to the patient that the next few minutes will be up-beat. You will be welcome — most welcome!

Your very presence indicates that you have hope for the patient. Express this hope by reassuring the bed-ridden that he or she, has been in your thoughts. Tell of others who are concerned, and have asked about the sick one. How comforting for a patient to know that many friends are concerned. This good news, from outside the hospital, can give a boost to the spirits. Bring these "good tidings" in a natural way to get your visit off to a good start.

Following up on this initial thrust of hope into the patient's life, search for other hope-sources. Perhaps a mutual friend, or a friend of a friend, has had a successful recovery from a similar illness. Telling these experiences will make the flame of hope burn brighter. Hope of recovery can be achieved easier than faith in recovery. Hope is a desire accompanied by some degree of expectation. If, when you witness, you can fan this flicker of hope, your visit will be a four-star effort. Anticipation that one will get well may shorten the illness. Hope for hope!

To get the patient in a hope-filled frame of mind, you must make clear your own strong hope. Don't be hopeful without a cause. Don't express your hopefulness in a manner that suggests "wishful thinking." You can use thoughts such as, "You have every reason to be hopeful"; "I wouldn't be surprised if you're back home in a week or so." Be intelligent about a comment like this, but be sure to make it. Keep alive your own hope. Then relay it, with all the conviction you have, into the mind of the patient. With both the patient and you building up a positive expectation, there's no telling how surprising the benefits might be.

This "holding on to hope" should extend to all the patient's visitors. When you talk to friends of the patient, be hope-filled. Some well-meaning persons tend to dramatize all illness. They exaggerate the depressing appearance of the patient. You know the type. Many times they "bring the hearse right up to the door" in describing what they saw. What possible good can this accomplish? If you are appalled by the patient's appearance remain silent. Hold on to your optimism. Be positive. Let mutual friends know you are optimistic and encourage them to be likewise. When the patient becomes exposed to multiple visitor optimism, hope that it will be contagious. This witness of optimism can be powerful.

Sometimes, you can follow the doctor's example of encouragement. They know that a positive attitude helps implant a "will to recover." This is helpful in making the drugs and surgery work. Notice the doctor if he drops in during your visit. Nurses, too, are experts in the art of bringing hope to the patient. Have you ever wondered why this is so? They have seen what the medicine of hope does for the seriously ill. They hope, too. They, too, are relying on God to bring hope and health. Must be that it works!

Without doubt, it is true that doctors use hope wisely. They come to a realization of the value of hope. When treatment appears ineffective, when they are forced to go back to their books, they desperately hang on to hope. Hope is a feeling beyond fact. Hope is a divine heartbeat that gives life when human hearts faint. Hope is God, acting to prove to man that he should never give up. The medical profession, stripped of mysterious hopes, would be sapped of its vigor and growth. They know it.

There are many Christian doctors who become "extra special" to Christian patients. There are other doctors whose faith is less obvious, but whose hope and trust in the Divine is worn on their stethoscopes. In their caring, in their attitudes, in their competency, they exhibit a big "plus" to the patient. It is hard to imagine any doctor avowing to be an agnostic while being a spectator to the victories of hope and faith. As you visit the patient, you may become aware of the doctor's, or nurse's, apparent faith. If so, make it a must to relay these observations to your sick friend. How reassuring it is to the patient to realize there is a third party helping along — by the name of God!

Your witness of hope can touch all of those in the "sickness circle." The wives and husbands, brothers and sisters, relatives and friends are all grasping for hope. In this convulsion of caring, God is hard at work. While only one body may be savaged by sickness, numbers of others are distraught. They, too, need your optimism and hope. Like the pebble dropped into the water, the ripples created by your hopefulness spread out in circles to help others.

Have you ever wondered about the "why" of suffering? Consider its "multiple impacts" as possible reasons. You never know when your hopefulness for the patient may change the life of another in the sickness-circle. Not only at the bedside, but in the waiting room, the lounge, or the hospital cafeteria, you may be given opportunities to instill hope in others. There is a common need for hope among all those in a hospital. Let God help you exhibit hope and cheer to everyone you meet in the sanctuary-of-the-sick.

Generating Courage Within the Patient

It takes courage to face the pain and danger of illness. Your first emphasis is instilling hope to permit a calmness. After this, another giant step can be taken — a concentration on generating courage. It is the ability to boldly face what lies ahead. If you can implant courage, you are giving the patient dignity of spirit.

The quality of courage can make a telling difference. Much is said about dignity in death. Dignity in life can be equally, if not more, important. To suffer anxiety, fears, and pain with dignity is an achievement. Dignity of life under stress generates an admiration beyond description. If you can be responsible for the creation of but a tad of courage, the Lord, through the patient, will be glorified.

To encourage a sick person demands prayer and intelligence. This encouragement is possible only if you spend time in deep-gut prayer. There are no pat prayers or pat answers to this witnessing problem. No syndicated prayer for the sick will exercise the love of God. You may well have to wrench your spirit in groanings before the Lord will let you know that he is listening. If ever you get close to the beating heart of witness, it will be in the process of this intercessory prayer. When God gives courage to the patient, it is like a birth. The fears and pains fade in light of the joy.

While *hope* is primarily feeling, *encouragement* is essentially fact. When your witness provides both facts and feelings to the patient, it becomes whole. There exist a number of facts on which to base your encouragement witness: the reputation of the doctor, the competency of the nurses, the condition of the hospital, the sophistication of medical equipment, the efficiency of the intensive care area, statistics or other facts related to the patient's illness, the progress of medical research, the healing power of new medicines, good reports from other patients, and, you might think of still other encouragements you could add to this list. An array of encouraging evidence is not too difficult to find — and use.

How do you find this type of information? Much can be obtained through the simple steps of reading and asking questions. Perhaps you have a *Family Medical Guide* in your house. Check out the patient's illness. This will enable you to talk much more intelligently to the sufferer. Whatever you learn, use the facts in an encouraging and wise manner. Never lie about the seriousness of any situation, but try for an optimistic interpretation of the facts. Like a half glass of water: it can be described as half empty, or, better, half full!

Medical information, if not available in your home, is plentiful at your local library. Librarians will be glad to help you find just what you want. Another good source of encouraging facts is your church library. Many modern church libraries are gold mines of encouraging facts relating to the ill. Also, illnesses like cancer, heart attacks, stroke, MS or MD, have association offices in most cities that are eager to supply you with information. Acquaint yourself, as well as possible, with the facts, not the fables, of the sickness. Many times we learn, through well-meant but mistaken sources, all kinds of scary misinformation. By presenting encouraging, authentic facts to the patient, you will be genuinely helpful. However, it is imperative to remember you are not an M.D., and in no circumstances should you prognosticate or give medical advice.

Encouragement takes many forms. The parent-patient wants to be assured that the children are being cared for; that the household is being cleaned; that her or his spouse is managing in the patient's absence; that his or her many responsibilities are being met by family and friends. Bread-winners will be similarly concerned, but about some different situations. They need assurances about family, too. But they also worry about their jobs; and, naturally, the money to take care of the sickness. If you can reassure in any of these areas, you'll help erase worry. Some information is too personal, but even if you can fill in with only a general report, it will be appreciated.

Encouragement — the building up of patient courage — can become a group effort. Talk with other of the patient's visitors. Suggest that they, too, use some of the encouraging information you might have passed on. Hearing encouraging facts from one person is beneficial, but if the patient hears good news from two or more visitors, the helpful effects are multiplied. Even negative-type friends can be influenced to be more positive. The patient who gets courage-building thoughts from many sources is blessed.

Try to find out the patient's probable schedule of recovery. To reassure that "this too will pass" focuses the mind on the return to health. It makes present suffering more bearable. This gives the patient a happy, predictable end to the ordeal. What a boost! It is infinitely easier to face up to fears if the light at the end of the tunnel can be seen. So focus on this end-of-suffering. However, don't indulge in unrealistic thinking about an early discharge time — this could turn out to be more harmful than helpful.

The patient's fears are facts. They can best be overcome by other facts. Given the right kind of encouraging and accurate information, the patient can overcome much fear. Make sure of your facts and state them with conviction. Obviously, nothing is one hundred percent certain in any illness, so take a guarded-but-optimistic view. Make sure your facts are reliable. If possible, check the doctor or the chief nurse. You can make an outright request for optimistic information. Most of the time they are cooperative because they know a courageous attitude helps recovery.

A most successful courage-builder is to state, "This too will pass." For ninety-nine percent of the patients, relief is just a short time away. This is a fact. When you emphasize that within a few days, or weeks, the suffering will be gone, most patients brighten up. In this happy anticipation — based on fact — courage can be born. Once the patient focuses on a better tomorrow, courage will master the sufferings of the day.

Another courage-inspiring phrase is "take it one day at a time." Getting through the present day usually can be tolerated because the timespan is short. The one-day-at-a-time attitude permits the realization of step-by-step progress in the recovery. Today, a particular pain may stop — some equipment may be taken away — the doctor may have good news. These day-by-day steps toward recovery can build the courage needed.

In addition to words, consider the encouraging power of touch. Touching is a simple act of love. To many, it comes naturally. You can reach out for the hand of the sick one and gently squeeze it. Power seems to flow from the healthy body to the sick. It seems like the spirit of life becomes a current from one person to the other. The soothing of the brow, or the hair, can bring a touch of bliss. With loved ones, a gentle kiss means worlds. There are many ways to encourage through touching. This is one form of nonverbal help that your witness will find easy to carry out. It becomes love-in-action.

Your encouragement becomes a double benefit when you

follow through after the patient's hospital discharge. If the recovery is long-term, there might be a slackening off of visits. Your witness gathers strength when you follow up with regular get-togethers. The convalescent patient is usually out of danger, is more optimistic, but still needs encouragement. A prolonged recovery period can be rough. There is the danger of self-pity if the return to full health is slow. Arrange fairly regular visits, even if you can't stay long. Make sure the patient feels your continued and genuine concern.

If you cannot make as many visits as you would like, cheer up the convalescent with "get well cards." There are literally hundreds of cards, sparkling with good thoughts, that you can use. In fact, if you alternate a card with a visit, you may lend extra excitement. Cards are sometimes expensive, so also consider writing short notes of encouragement. Many cards give you the additional opportunity of bringing a bit of Scripture to attention. If you write a note, a simple "God bless you" stamps your thoughts as Christian.

Encouragement springs from verbal expressions, nonverbal actions, use of cards, personal memos, and small gifts. There seems to be something special about the gift of flowers. Flowers have a God-given ability to turn thoughts to the beauty of life. Even "hard shell" men find a gift of flowers a real "pick up." It doesn't seem to matter if it is a single bloom picked from a home garden, or a florist's masterpiece; the gift of flowers is an appreciated expression of tender caring.

If you know the patient well, bring some small gift that relates to a particular hobby or interest. For instance, one person might be happy with a small book of poetry or an inspirational plaque — another with a sports magazine. Many inexpensive, yet meaningful, items are displayed in the hospital's gift store. Use of scriptural tracts and artifacts can also be considered. However, you should be careful about blatantly proselyting messages; rather, select a communication of loving encouragement. Use your good judgment.

Evidences of encouragement, on your part, can be extended to the entire family of the patient. At times, they suffer as much as, or more than, the patient. Illnesses bring changes in the lives of those surrounding the patient. It is hard to overestimate the impact on the mother and father of a small child desperately ill — of the heart-searching of a family when a father's or mother's life is threatened — or the impact on fellow students when a classmate is crippled. Your sharing, to all influenced, will be remembered for years. In the arena of illness, God truly works in mysterious ways.

As you transmit courage to patient, family, and friends alike, you become fused with God's love. Your caring exposes its depth. If you take on the suffering of your sick friends, you mirror God's love. You can instill *hope* and, you can give *encouragement*.

Truthfully Comforting the Patient

Hope and *encouragement* become comforting only if the patient believes you are truthful. Put yourself in the patient's position to grasp the problem. It is so easy to discount your visits as just well-intentioned conversation. Or, your notes, cards, and gifts as simply a show of civility. What is needed is "proof" — something that proves your bottom-line truthfulness — a strong "clincher" upon which the patient can rely. Only then will you really comfort.

What would be the strongest possible "clincher" you could use? It's an actual experience from your own life. It's powerful because an experience cannot be denied. It stands as proof that what you said was true. It is, in essence, a "guarantee" of your reliability. If you have had the same illness as the patient, you can be assured of a rapt audience. Second best, if you are familiar with someone else who suffered the patient's illness, your views will carry conviction. Using real-life experiences of identical, or similar, recoveries sets you on solid ground.

If the patient has cancer, your views are respected if you, too, have suffered the same illness, and this promotes acceptance of your encouragements. There's a good chance that you have had other experiences similar to the patient's. As you get older, it becomes more probable that you could personally relate this way to any number of health problems. This fosters acceptance for, and comfort from, all that you say.

It's wise to be careful when you make this personal type of affirmation. If you unduly emphasize your experience, you may become guilty of a common malady — "one-upmanship" of the patient's suffering. If you dwell on the greater degree of suffering you went through, you are not showing proper caring. Describe just enough of your experience to convince the patient that you're not "talking through your hat" — but that you really understand.

The bottom line in a strong affirmation is to simply state how God helped you. Then, make a flat-out statement that you believe God can do the same for the patient. Your experience, plus your affirmation, will carry conviction. This type of boldness can bring to the ill a lessening of anxiety — a renewal of personal faith — a depth of comfort.

Have no fear about your ability to make this kind of bold witness. Anybody can make a statement about their experiences with God. Often this brings a visible upsurge in the patient's morale. Perhaps you will have the joy of experiencing, as I have had, patients whose eyes will well up with tears of appreciation. Or, the reaching out to you as a "thanks" for what you've said. They will know you are affirming — through actual life experiences — the love of God that can be theirs, too. What comfort!

While the sickness is confined to one person, your sick-witness will not escape the attention of visitors. In a sense, visitors are patients also. They suffer many of the fears of the patient. The loved ones suffer before the operation — after the operation — and during the patient's recovery. While only one patient-body may be ravaged, numbers of friend's souls are shaken. Wives, husbands, brothers, sisters, mothers, fathers, relatives, and friends are part of this "circle of caring." We do not yet understand all the "why's" of sickness. We do know that when it occurs, God is at work in the hearts of many. Could this be one reason for sickness?

As the patient is helped, it is probable that others are also benefitting. The question, "Why did this happen?" occurs to patient and friends alike. God pulls all of us "up short." We tend to re-examine our attitudes and beliefs. In the sanctuary called "hospital," new decisions are reached. New commitments are made. The longer we travel on life's highway, the clearer it becomes that these "hospital detours" have telling effects. Your presence, your attitudes, and your caring for one ill person may touch many. Your Christianity spreads in all directions, like ripples spreading when a stone is dropped in still water.

There comes the time when you think about bringing your visit to an end. Leaving is important. Even if your visit is concluded promptly, if it does not express love, it means little. A two-hour visit, consisting of meaningless chit-chat has small value. Ten minutes of real encouragement and affirmation is priceless. Love the patient, and be patient in loving.

The best expressions of love are short and sincere. Try not to be overly emotional. The emotional defenses of the sick are thin. You've noticed how easily a weakened person is prone to tears and fears. Show your love without taxing either the patient or yourself. Quiet appreciation will grow long after the visit is over. Little kindnesses, offered at the sickbed, have a tendency to grow in importance.

What are some expressions of love you can exhibit before saying "Goodbye and God bless you?" There are many. These few may generate many more:

Ask if there is anything you can do, either at the hospital or at home, for the patient. Some little chore, such as watering plants, or picking up mail, may loom large in the mind of the ill one.

See if you can check with the family of the patient to see if they need anything. Tell the patient you'd like to be helpful.

Make an offer of soup, or other food for the patient (if allowed), or the family.

Check and see if you can bring some "diversionary" material the next time you come. Crossword puzzles, books, tracts, and one-person games can keep the mind off the illness. Let the patient know you'll contact a prayer group. It is not critical that the denomination be the same as the patient's.

If you know the patient intimately, you could ask if help would be welcome on special, personal aspects of family life. Baby-sitting, informing certain neighbors, contacting family members, or any of a score of highly personal problems need solving.

If you're both working at the same place of business, be sure to inform other employees. Spread the news around with a hint that cards, (or a group card), would be welcome. Also, (if the patient doesn't mind), give out the hospital room number. Inquire of the patient whether there is anything, or anybody, at the place of work, whom you might particularly inform or instruct.

If feasible, you might ask if there are any financial details with which you could assist at the bank, or through the mail.

From this beginning, you can enlarge your list of helps. Keep in mind the story of the Good Samaritan. While you may be thinking in terms of spiritual needs, be sure to help with tangible needs. Care on the practical level is a priority. Addressing these practical needs, with practical deeds, becomes proof that your spiritual viewpoints are not hollow words. Deeds give the necessary quality to your witness.

Before you make your actual exit, if you can find the courage, simply say, "Why don't we have a short prayer?" It is likely that the patient will agree and bow. Then, in just a very few words, express the hope that is in God:

> *Father, you have told us that nothing can separate (name) from the love of God in Christ Jesus. In His name we ask for comfort and recovery for (name). Thank you Lord.*

Use your own words. Keep it short. Mean every word of it. Then leave.

Chapter 8

"I Found a Way to Rev up Our Pastor"

It almost shocked me off the pew! Of course, it happened many years ago, when I had but a few witnessing experiences, so I can claim some excuse. My good Christian friend bowled me over when she said, "Why don't you witness to our pastor?"

At the time, it never occurred to me that our pastor needed any help, whatsoever, from a member of the laity. The other way around I could understand. My good friend, whose father was a minister, truly opened my eyes. That day she graciously let me in on what seems to be a big secret. It was that ministers have the same fears, doubts, and discouragements that we all have! But, they are under great disadvantage. Their position implies a spiritual strength that is beyond the need of our help. In most cases, their desire for love is greater than that of their members, for they must meet unbelievable testing and trial.

You and I, when ministering to our pastor, have the opportunity to improve the entire congregation. When we encourage our pastor, with love and deeds, we complete a cycle-of-caring that involves the entire church. Because congregations are human, they are not always logical or forgiving. With tongue in cheek, just consider the following:

If the pastor is young, they say he lacks experience; if he's old, he's "over the hill."
If he has five or six children, he has too many; if he has none, he's selfish.
If he preaches from notes, he's boring; if he's extemporaneous, he's shallow.
If he caters to the poor, he's wasting valuable effort; if he caters to the rich, he's playing politics.
If he uses anecdotes, he's neglecting the Scripture; if he doesn't, he isn't interesting.
If he preaches guilt, he's harmful; if he doesn't, he's compromising.

If he sticks to the Bible, he's too narrow; if he interprets, he's too liberal.

If he doesn't please everybody, he should leave; if he does, he's wishy-washy.

If he drives an old car, it's disgraceful; if he drives a new one, it's ostentatious.

If he preaches all the time, he's pulpit possessive; if he invites guest preachers, he's a shirker.

If he gets a large salary, he's mercenary; if a small one, he isn't worth even that.

— anonymous

It's no wonder that pastors just can't win! If you think they have trouble pleasing the congregation, pause a moment over the problems of their spouses. They have to be saints. There are few positions, in all of life, that are more vulnerable to criticism. Contrary to common belief, life in the ministry is not for sissies. It takes a thick skin, plenty of courage, and super-stamina to make a success of the pastoral team. Were it not for the constant help of the Holy Spirit, the supply of clergy would simply dry up. This makes it a "must" that you and I witness to our pastors, their spouses, even their children.

For some years, now, I have observed the refreshing effects of love deeds toward ministers. To revitalize your pastor, there are three simple steps. You can identify them by the acronym REV, which is easy to remember, and effective when applied. Without embarrassment or aggressiveness, REV will help to spiritually REVitalize your pastorate by:

*R*eassuring!

*E*ncouraging!

*V*aluing!

Reassuring Your Pastor

Acknowledging past success is always appreciated. What puts power into your witness happens to be a great deal more than, "good sermon this morning, pastor." The Sunday morning reassurance is helpful to the pastor (and sometimes his or her attending spouse), but is a small first step. Besides the one hour on Sunday morning, there are 167 hours left in every week in which to give a reassuring word. You see your minister and family at worship services, Bible study groups, fellowship meetings, socials, committee meetings, and perhaps even on the street. Every meeting is an opening for you to be reassuring. You can congratulate him on his sermons, prayers, visitations, policies, programs, or other facets of his spiritual or personal life.

Even if he appears confident as the Rock of Gibraltar, your minister has a deep need to be reassured. It takes a lot of reassurance to counteract the criticism most pastors suffer. There must exist some obscure natural law that makes one critical remark stronger than ten words of praise. Many a minister has been thrown into depression by the sniping of inconsiderate parishioners. The effect is hard on the pastor and his or her family. The female pastor, usually battling for acceptance, has a particularly tough time with added criticism. You, and I, in our love, should counterbalance this negativism with large doses of REV.

Does this mean we can never criticize our pastor's actions? Hardly. If the minister received no criticism whatsoever, there would be a suspicion that the congregation wasn't concerned. Or worse, he was not challenging the members to reach out to their full potential. Members' questioning of certain actions can be constructive. It is the manner in which disagreement is put that becomes most important. Criticism, given in helpfulness, can become praise. Successful managers of people have learned how to do this. You'll actually be encouraging through suggesting alternative actions. When you disagree, don't "fly off the handle." Carefully work out positive alternatives and offer them as improvements. This type of criticism then becomes constructive witnessing.

If you are in agreement with your pastor, there are plenty

of reassuring opportunities. As a starter list, work on the following:

Reassure your pastor that the sermon was good. Be honest, fair, not "flowery."

Reassure your pastor that the content of a prayer was meaningful to you. Say it only if you mean it.

Reassure your pastor that special efforts, on a specific project or program, are appreciated.

Reassure your pastor when his or her family is winning the admiration of the congregation.

Reassure your pastor that good things are being said about his or her work.

Reassure your pastor of successful efforts to increase benevolence giving.

Reassure your pastor that her or his youth programs are making an impact on the youngsters.

Reassure your pastor, at the busy seasons of Christmas and Easter, that that extra work is being noticed.

Obviously important for these, and any other reassurances, is their honesty. It is better not to praise if you do not feel it is one-hundred percent true. Most ministers know how to separate courteous gestures from deeply-felt comments. It doesn't hurt to be courteous to your pastor, but it means so much more if your reinforcing word reflects deep conviction. So often, you've probably noted, pastors are not sincerely thanked. Criticism is easy to generate, praise is harder to come by. Let's fix that.

Have you ever tried to put yourself in your minister's shoes? It isn't easy, but it is an exercise in reality. No member agrees completely with everything the pastor is doing. Your reassurances on the work you find acceptable will give him a big lift. Pastors take comments of their members most seriously. The thrust of their efforts many times are the result of these comments. Where you agree, a witness of reassurance can have an uplifting effect on the entire congregation.

To be of maximum help, some members make a list of church efforts during the recent past. They go the whole gamut, from large scale stewardship program to small spiritual courtesy. If you'll do this, one or more of your pastor's efforts will strike you as being worthy of reassuring comment. Then, don't procrastinate. The very next time you talk to your pastor, reassure him. Tell him that this action was just great. Being extra-aware of your pastor's efforts will soon become automatic. You will soon have your own private list of good deeds deserving a reassuring word. This "reassuring witness" will then become an important part of your life. An enjoyable part.

Reassurances, by their nature, are inclined toward past performances. What about present and future actions? How can your witness improve your pastor's current work? One tested way is by being encouraging.

Encouraging Your Pastor

Sincere encouragement is a proven path to a more abundant witness for you; and, a more productive life for your minister. It may be hard for you to grasp this at first blush. Why, you might ask, do I have to reverse roles and minister to my pastor? Isn't he supposed to be in a better spiritual position then I? If a pastor, with his continuing walk with God, is so needful of encouragement, isn't something seriously wrong? Not at all! In fact, the more spiritually knowledgeable your pastor may be, the more encouragement he may need.

Knowledge can be likened to throwing a pebble into still waters. It activates waves which spread out in a 360 degree circle. A small pebble will create small waves. The larger the pebble, the larger the waves created. Imagine the pond of still water being the total of knowledge. Your personal intelligence is represented by the pebble. As your intelligence splashes into the pond of knowledge, its waves spread out to touch knowledge not known. The larger the pebble of your intelligence, the bigger waves it causes, which then touch greater areas of unknown knowledge. It follows that the more you know, the more you know you don't know.

The spiritual knowledge of our pastors touches increasingly larger areas of the unknown. This realization can be sobering. Your pastor can become acutely aware of the vastness of his ignorance. It can cause doubts, serious anxieties, and a need for much encouragement. It is in these circumstances that your encouragement can be a wonder-witness. It serves to help your pastor cope with his feelings of mental and spiritual inferiority. It can be exactly what is most needed to help him personally, and also the congregation at large.

You can be sure that your pastor is not only aware of his ministering shortcomings, but also of his sins and errors. There once existed the idea that ministers were a spiritual cut above normal human beings. The ministry itself perpetuated this idea. It seemed necessary to project an image of spiritual superiority. It was thought that this stance would benefit the church. As the Twentieth Century rolled along, with its world wars, technological breakthroughs, and social revolutions, more and more pastors were forced to re-examine this public posture. You have probably noted, as certainly as I, that it is now not at all unusual for a contemporary pastor to publicly admit his errors. Ripping away this veil of professional righteousness has vastly improved communications between pastors and their flocks. It's wonderful for you and me to be assured that we all stumble, that we all are no more, or no less, than saved sinners.

One of the greatest preachers of all time, the apostle Paul, confessed, in Romans 7:

For I delight in the law of God, after the inward man; but I see another law in my members, warring against the law of my mind,

and bringing me into captivity to the law of sin which is in my members.
Oh wretched man that I am! Who shall deliver me from the body of this death?
I thank God through Jesus Christ our Lord. So with the mind I myself serve the law of God; but with the flesh the law of sin.

This, from Paul, gives cause for the ministry to be totally honest with themselves and their congregations. It is no easy confession, on the part of either the pastor or layperson, to face these facts. Your pastor, whether it appears so or not, needs your encouragement. She needs to know that you encourage the ideas, plans, and programs she is pushing. She needs to know that you have enthusiasm for her work. She needs to feel that you are with her, and her work.

Another exciting step in encouraging your pastor is prayer. With it, you can witness silently, even your pastor will not know. Yet, the Holy Spirit will consider your every request, helping to honor them for your pastor's welfare. I cannot prove it, but I have been aware that some pastors I have prayed for sensed what I was doing. And, without even a hint from me. The same can be true for you. As your witness of prayer continues, I can almost guarantee you'll notice a new warmth and love growing between you. You'll notice something else, too. Your own enthusiasm will increase. It tends to be contagious, too; you'll sense changed attitudes among church members. Prayer seems to act like a balm on the sores of the church and its pastor.

While praying is effective, there are several other gentle encouragements. If the pastor announces a new sermon series, and you feel it will be interesting, make sure to tell him. It's such a simple encouragement. It may be that he is just waiting for this one word of support to give him a needed boost. Or, after a congregational or officers' meeting, a few words of encouragement about an item will fall like welcomed rain. It need not happen inside the church. If you meet your pastor socially, or even out on the street, make sure you encourage him about his ideas. The place is not important, the encouragement is all-important.

One of the most telling times to encourage your pastor is following the annual congregation meeting. Here, she usually submits her goals for the coming year. Even if you don't agree with all her ideas, make sure to encourage her on the ones you favor. The planning for the year ahead probably has her weary. Anxiety builds up and takes its toll. Write down in red ink to absolutely, positively encourage her on all the ideas which you favor. Her feelings of accomplishment will brighten. Her enthusiasm will heighten. You, too, will feel extra good.

Another encouraging way to witness is to help the pastor meet his leadership responsibilities. Make every effort in helping select new church officers. Your assistance in finding these appointments can take much weight off his weary shoulders. As you report on possible officer material things will happen to your witness. Before long you will find your pastor depending on you as a source of good officer nominees. If elected, the capable persons you helped select will give you satisfaction — even joy.

There exists one area of encouragement surprisingly neglected. I would not hesitate a moment to suggest that encouraging the pastor's spouse should be on top of your supportive witness. In most congregations, the pastor's spouse is the most visible, criticized, and vulnerable person of all. Her or his efforts with the membership of the church usually are the key to a successful ministry. The minister, himself, may find professional acceptance: but, unless his spouse is similarly embraced by the congregation, there will be difficulties. What a trial this can become to a sensitive minister's husband or wife! Yet, what an opportunity for you.

Easy as falling off a log, one of the best ways to help is simply to repeat what you've said to the pastor. You may be assured that your pastor and his spouse talk over their every problem. Like most couples, they lean heavily on each other for honest reactions. Any encouragement given to one is quickly shared with the other. Repeating your satisfactions about the pastor's work to his or her spouse has a reinforcing effect. As they tell each other of your identical comments, their importance is enhanced. Voila! You have made both happy!

Another positive area for encouragement is the spouse's work with the congregation. The pastor's spouse has heavy responsibility in this area. Depending on the church, and her or his personal philosophy, the pastor's husband or wife can play that role in a number of ways. Many tend to become the "leading layperson," or at the least, the visible example of how other church laypersons should act. Being in this kind of a "fish bowl," she or he generates constant comment, and needs encouragement whenever it can be given. Make sure you give your pastor's spouse a hearty "pat on the back," often.

It seems that a new commandment is in order, "love your pastor's spouse as yourself." To play the role of the nit-picking critic does not reflect the compassion of a true Christian. We all realize it's impossible to agree one-hundred percent with somebody else's views. How loving it becomes when you overlook petty differences and actively encourage all those efforts with which you agree. Once again, this encouragement will get back to the pastor and both members of the pastor-team will benefit. All this "double witness" requires is concern and compassion.

Some laypersons have difficulty talking with their pastor's spouse. There are several reasons; one hindrance springs from the position itself, which some members tend to unduly revere. This restricts natural communications. There is also an inhibition to talk based on the notion that the pastor's spouse is some sort of spiritual "royalty." All of these conditions can be overcome, and should be. The pastor's spouse is a long-suffering, understanding, normal human being, who needs Christian love and encouragement like all of us. Her or his work with the membership of the church deserves your finest cooperation.

When encouraging words about the pastor/spouse ministerial team are shared with other church members, good things happen. As an indirect type of encouragement, shared praise gets back to the pastoral family circle. Imagine how thrilled they are when they hear, through a third party, that you have spoken encouragingly about their efforts. In some ways, this relayed praise is the most beneficial because it involves more people. It can spread out and embrace many members of the church. It builds unity and joy. It becomes a positive witness in ever-widening circles.

In overview: as the pastor, spouse, their ministry, and visions for your church are encouraged, the result is constant improvement. It follows that being encouraged in positive efforts, they diligently seek even greater progress. As the years go by, you will be able to sit back and, with satisfaction, reflect on these improvements. Your reassurances of past efforts, and encouragements of present actions, lead to an overall awareness of your church's place in the plan of God. This appreciation of the pastor/spouse team can become the strong third leg of your witness effort to your pastor.

Valuing Your Pastor

This is the strong, silent witness at your command. You may well, somewhere along the way, begin to place a high value on the position of your pastor. It may be triggered by some act of love on her part. Or, some courageous stand for a principle. In a general way, it may slowly dawn on you that your pastor is "something else," overcoming one obstacle after another. If you are honest with yourself, you will admit that the ministry has a value far beyond the ordinary. And, so should it be treated. In so admiring it, beyond normal bounds, you will discover witnessing vitality.

The more you value your pastor/spouse team, the more

constructive will be your attitude. As with anything we value, the way we speak, defend, and praise them, will reflect our conviction of their quality. They will get "top reviews" when you are asked what you think. You won't "gush over" in your evaluation, but your positive evaluation of their work will be given with enthusiasm. Can you honestly avoid this? Don't try, for this practice will give power to your witness. It seems like all products and services in modern life are evaluated and promoted. Whatever your enthusiastic evaluations of the work of your pastor/spouse team, they will be contemporary and proper.

It would be safe to say that your pastor seldom blows her own horn. A minister rarely brags. Perhaps the closest thing to personal praise is a sharing of some success at a previous pastorate. When this is given, it is to help the present congregation in some way. As with M. D.s, lawyers, and other professionals, a modest attitude demands respect. Let us dig up the many reasons we should respect, and value, our pastor. Here are a few:

1. Ordained ministers spend long, hard years in higher education preparing themselves. Educational requirements have become increasingly tough. The sacrifices made to become a minister deserve our recognition.

2. The special discipline demanded by pastoral work is apparent. Selecting the ministry is never taken lightly. Some believe they are "called," others struggle through much self-examination. This commitment to discipline earns respect.

3. The responsibility of being the spiritual leader for hundreds, or perhaps thousands, of church members is hard to imagine. If the physician's work with the body is respected, how much greater should we value our minister's work with the soul.

4. Preaching is essential to our personal faith. Romans 10:14 states: "And how shall they believe in Him of whom they have not heard? And how shall they hear without a preacher?" What value to us!

5. Pastors, as a group, are wonderful people. Consider Romans 10:15: "As it is written, how beautiful are the feet of them that preach the gospel of peace, and bring glad tidings of good things!" Certainly, this could be the origination of the phrase, "the beautiful people." Yes, pastors are to be admired.

There are strictly private reasons why you might want to honor your pastor. He may have a style to his preaching that "fits you to a T!" I shall never forget a personal experience in a large Michigan church. The quote over its entranceway was, "A House of Prayer for All People." The Senior Pastor reinforced this idea with constant words of comfort. You could not listen to a single sermon without feeling the touch of the Comforter. Talk about valuing a pastor: the members pushed and shoved to gain the best pews whenever he preached. These strictly private preferences can be most important in placing value on your pastor.

In a worldly vein, you and I can readily see the "human being" in the minister. There is no perfect preacher. There is no perfect church member. Like all of us, pastors are human; they sin, procrastinate, lack faith, lack courage, struggle with their shortcomings. It helps us recognize that there are weaknesses in all people. Happily, this makes it possible to relate to one another, the pastor to us — we to the pastor. As you and I understand these weaknesses, we grow in the ability to forgive. As we forgive, we make room for the Holy Spirit to dominate more of our life. How revealing is Paul's description of his own preaching, as recorded in 1 Corinthians 2:1-5:

And I, brethren, when I came to you, came not with excellence of speech or of wisdom, declaring into you the testimony of God.
For I determined not to know anything among you, save Jesus Christ, and Him crucified.
And I was with you in weakness, and in fear, and in much trembling.
And my speech and my preaching was not with enticing words of man's wisdom, but in demonstration of the Spirit and of power.
That your faith should not stand in the wisdom of men, but in the power of God.

These words sing! They proclaim that the preacher put

down his own wisdom to focus on the power of God. The power of God is exclusive. Only it can give, develop, and perfect a soul-saving sermon. There exists a human "excellency of speech or of wisdom"; but it is secondary. The words of men such as Neibauer, Barth, or Muggeridge thrill us with their insight; but the "rubber hits the road" only when the power of God puts faith into being. No value placed on a pastor's work is too great if you can sense the existence and power of the Holy Spirit in his preaching.

Your expressions of the value and worthiness of your pastor's work are sure to take hold in your congregation. Given with enthusiasm and conviction, these expressions tend to multiply. Others will pick up your spirit of admiration, and the morale of the entire church will be boosted. It does not take many to influence the outlook of an entire congregation. Neither does it take a long time. Placing a true and constructive valuation on your pastor is a witness often overlooked. Putting "valuation" into practice can be one of the most constructive of your witnesses.

How easy it becomes to REV up your pastor. How effective! Equally important, this is a witnessing procedure that finds acceptance among even the most shy of Christians. Review, in your own mind how you can start to:

*R*eassure your pastor on his or her past efforts.
*E*ncourage your pastor on present and future work.
*V*alue your pastor's work as you speak to others.

It is not unusual for a wave of growth to wash over a congregation when the pastor becomes an object of witness. As appreciation builds; as endorsements of his planning, preaching, praying, visiting, counseling, and administering mount up; faces and hearts in the congregation take on new expressions. The presence of the Holy Spirit is felt. An aura of love glows around the people and the building. The power of God and his Gospel ring out more clearly. An attitude of joy begins to take over. You can be responsible for this "miracle." Oh, what power you have! Why not start to use it — now.

Chapter 9

"Can I Bring an Outsider In?"

Deep down in your heart you yearn to bring an "outsider" into the church. You probably feel that if you could help just one who is lost come into the fellowship of the church, your witnessing effort would be a triumph. This, you're sure, would represent God's highest use of your life. Yet, this fundamental evangelizing staggers you. You cannot see, within your own capabilities, how it can be accomplished. But, there is reason to believe, nothing is farther from the truth. Believe this. Believe that you can become an evangelist — that you can help bring outsiders in — believe it because it is not nearly as hard as you think!

You probably have an opinion that bringing outsiders into the church requires courage and knowledge far beyond your reach. You simply cannot see yourself, as some would have you believe is necessary, walking down "skid row," barging into a saloon, facing up to a drunken customer, and leading him through the doors of your church. If this is what it takes to be a genuine evangelist, millions upon millions of Christian ministers, officers, and lay persons never will qualify. In fact, it is this concept that has short-circuited Christian witnessing activity for hundreds of years.

Let's start at the beginning. Let's ask ourselves, "Who are the outsiders?" Are those outside the Christian church primarily alcoholics, prostitutes, and criminals? The answers have been given by a man who has been aptly described as one of the greatest evangelists of our time. He is George Gallup, Jr., son of the founder of the Gallup Poll. More than any other living person, he, through his pioneering scientific research, has documented "The Unchurched American." Through prodigious studies at the Princeton Religion Research Center, America's unchurched have been defined and profiled.

Gallup has provided the Christian church with new directions. Further, he has held on to objectivity, avoiding the emphases of any one denomination.

In his work are discovered answers to questions like:

"Are the people outside the church atheists?"
"Do these outsiders ever think of God?"
"What do they believe about Jesus Christ?"
"What do they think of the Bible?"
"Why don't they want to go to church?"
"Were they church-going people as children?"

Once you get the answers to these questions, you will begin to realize that bringing outsiders into a believing fellowship is possible. However, it will take new means, new approaches, a dramatic change in witnessing. Sooner or later, you will run into persons who confide that they "don't attend church." These "outsiders," we have discovered, have some remarkable opinions and beliefs. Here are some of Gallup's startling findings about those who have no church connection:

How Many Are There?
For years religious and secular estimates of the number of unchurched varied widely. Many of the estimates were either hopeful guesses, or deliberate propaganda. Speakers would use figures to suit their purposes, safe from being seriously challenged. It probably was this fact that initially led Dr. Gallup to originate his research on the unchurched.

Using all the facilities and experience of the Princeton research complex, he originated the first truly scientific, in-depth study of the unchurched. His findings are recognized as singularly authentic. In America, in the 1980's, there are some 61,000,000 adults who are not members of any church. At the same moment in time, there are 141,000,000 adults who are church members. Effectively, then, for every unchurched adult, there are two and one-third churched adults.

Of these 61,000,000 "outsiders," Gallup found that one-third, roughly 20,000,000, were Jews, members of other major religions such as Islam, or self-proclaimed atheists. The astounding fact was that the two-thirds majority of the non-churched were Christians. This amounts to some 40,000,000 American Christians who are not members of any Christian church. This is the primary audience for our witnessing. In order to approach them in the most intelligent manner, we should know as much as we can about their attitudes toward, and beliefs about, the church.

What Do They Believe Concerning the Bible?

Because the Bible is the source of our beliefs, what non-church members believe about it is of top importance. It is precisely how much of the Bible they believe which dictates how we go about winning them to the church. And, fortunately, Gallup's findings in this area give us reason to rejoice.

The research uncovered the surprising fact that twenty-seven percent of all "outsiders" believe the Bible is the actual word of God and is to be taken literally, word for word. Add to this another forty-three percent who believe the Bible is the inspired word of God. Finally, some ten percent simply do not know what they believe about the Bible. Added together, it amounts to eighty percent, or 48,000,000, of the non-churched who are "wide open" to our Christian witness. (Even the remaining twenty percent, about 12,000,000, who feel the Bible is a book of legends and moral perceptions, are not beyond our approach.)

Ten, or so, years ago, few in the ministry and fewer in the ranks of laypersons, could even imagine this broad an acceptance of the Bible.

What Do The Unchurched Think Of Jesus?

An astounding sixty-four percent of the unchurched declare

that Jesus Christ is "God, or the Son of God." This belief in Christ is the very foundation of salvation. Some 39,000,000, or almost two-thirds of the outsiders, can be considered as Christians — though unchurched.

An even higher percentage, sixty-eight percent, believe in the resurrection of Christ. The resurrection is the very heart of a Christian's faith in Christ as Lord, and the overwhelming majority of outsiders believe in this key fact. Surely, you and I must come to the conclusion that the majority of outsiders are already Christians.

Translating these beliefs into spiritual activity, almost one-half the outsiders state that they pray — everyday! Previously, we were led to suspect that the unchurched did not pray at all. Perhaps they did only in the case of great danger or catastrophe. How wrong we have been. There is some doubt that Christian church members pray as much.

What Do The Unchurched Think Of The Church?

To the unchurched, the "rubber hits the road" not when you bring up the Bible or Christ, but when you discuss the corporate church. This is what truly separates the Christians of America. The majority of the unchurched feel strongly that the church on earth, created and administered by human hands, actually is a spiritual hindrance.

Once again, Gallup shocks us by discovering that eight out of ten outsiders feel that a person can be a good Christian (or Jew) if he or she doesn't attend any church at all. This anti-church attitude runs even deeper. Eighty-six percent of the unchurched feel that, "an individual should arrive at his or her own religious beliefs independent of any religious institution.

While almost eighty percent of the unchurched have had some kind of religious training during their childhood, sixty percent think most churches have lost the real spiritual part of religion, fifty percent think most churches are not effective in helping people find the meaning of life, and thirty-six percent think that churches are not warm and accepting of outsiders.

Now we are zeroing in on the big difference between the churched and the unchurched. This has never been realized before. The *big* differences are not related to the Bible, God, or Christ. They are deep-seated differences relating to the corporate church. The unchurched, through life experiences, believe in the promises of God, but not the promises of the church-on-earth.

It is these beliefs of the unchurched that demand a dramatic shift away from most present day evangelizing. To be sure, there is a twenty-five percent minority of the unchurched who do not believe in God and Christ. For these, the "how to be saved" message is necessary. But, for every one of these persons (Jews, Moslems, atheists, agnostics), there are four others who cry out for answers to the question, "Why should I go to church?" This is the witnessing challenge of our times. This is your witnessing charge. Today! Now!

When you have an unchurched person confiding in you, or asking for answers about the church, you should first admit all the shortcomings. Don't try to be a purist; don't try to become a hero. Above all, don't insist the church is infallible. It isn't. So, disarm the unchurched, take the wind out of their sails at the start. You might have some trouble with these "confessions" about the church — but study them, and use as many as you can in good conscience. They will disarm many of the unchurched, and open them up to considering reasons for getting back into the church.

Indicate that these are some seldom discussed "confessions" of the church:

1. You don't have to belong to a church to be a Christian.
2. You can be a saved Christian without church membership.
3. Whether you're a church member or not, your good works will not save you.

108

4. Prayers, of members or non-members, are equally effective.

5. Church members are not "better" than non-church members.

6. Church members and non-church members are the same — sinners who are saved by the grace of God.

7. Both church members, and non-church members, are hypocritical — to about the same degree.

8. Churches need money to function — just like any other organization — including the family.

9. Neither the church, nor Christ, promises you riches, health, or happiness — but faith, hope, and love.

If you can have a discussion on any one, or all, of these "confessions," you are half-way home in making a positive witness. Persons outside the church do not expect such candor. Because of their opposition to the church, they create a hostile defense on the part of the church member. With more heat than light, these chats can end up mighty feisty. No progress is made. If there is blame for this sad outcome, the church member should assume it. We know better. And, only by this attitude can we show compassion and consideration.

Of course many of the outsider's concepts are wrong. But instead of bluntly challenging them, admit your inability to handle them. Better yet, if a truthful criticism is made, make sure you agree with it. Indicate you, too, are aware of the condition, and are trying to do something about it in your own church. Tell the outsider that he or she is intelligent enough to spot a condition that everybody agrees needs fixing. We're all on the same side — the side of truth.

Gallup indicates that most outsiders have strong feelings concerning three important beliefs about the present day church. These are:

1. The church has lost the real spiritual part of religion.

   2. The church is ineffective in helping find the real meaning of life.
   3. The church is "cold" to outsiders.

Every one of these objections is true in some church. And, every one is false in some other church. The point is that churches are not alike. In fact, just like people, there are no two churches in the whole world exactly alike. The thought can be developed even further. There is no other person exactly the same as your husband, or your wife. You married because he or she was "one of a kind." And, you loved this. The fact that no other man or woman pleased you so much did not make you totally reject all the rest of mankind.

The solution to the problems relating to spirituality, meaningfulness, and friendliness is one of successfully searching. There is a church that will please the outsider you're witnessing to. The problems are individual. What is a lack of spirituality to one person is a blessing of dignity to another. What is a lack of meaningfulness to one person is a lack of comprehension to another. What is a lack of friendliness to one person is a protection of privacy to another. Somewhere there is a church that is just right for every outsider. But like a prospective husband or wife — it needs finding.

Nevertheless, the search for the "right" church must be realistic. There is no perfect husband. There is no perfect wife. There is no perfect church. But, there are some spouses and churches that come mighty close. The truth needs another expansion — there are no perfect church members, either. The miracle of the church is in its billions of imperfect members straining in imperfect ways, trying to please the only Perfect One — Jesus Christ.

As the outsider sees this drama, many times an incorrect conclusion is reached. It is that church members are trying to be "better" than others. And, members are seen as trying to bolster their egos because of their faith. This outsider concept gives rise to the idea of church members trying to be "holier than thou." What a burden for the church to carry.

Right off the bat it would be wise to admit some truth to this criticism. Yes, there are members, whom we all probably know, who flaunt their church membership — who pride themselves on their seemingly sinless lives — who would like everybody to believe that they, and their families, are simply beyond reproach. These are the self-righteous. They are a hindrance to God and the church alike. Some say they have deeply harmed the spreading of the Gospel of Jesus Christ over the centuries.

As a final admission of self-righteousness, you should confess its presence in some churches. Like individuals, churches can fall into the error of becoming self-elevating. The attitudes of its ministers, officers, and members, tell a sad story. Like some lodges, secret societies, and restricted clubs, these churches encourage an image of superiority. In fact, church public relations sometimes is "angled" to promote an image of extraordinary distinction. Bad enough for other church members, for outsiders this "pride of faith" is like a red flag. They want nothing to do with it. Do you blame them?

What is left to talk about? This admission of error after error of both the church and the Christian opens the mind and the heart of the outsider. By purging the conversation of false values, you are ready to get down to rock bottom. You will have stripped the church's image of both tinsel and tarnish. Once done, you need not exaggerate the qualities of the church nor its members. You and the outsider will both know better. You should be emptied of everything but a loving desire to be helpful. This is your task — to help outsiders know the truth. They will make up their own minds.

The final work with an outsider, after you have discussed the church and its members in general, is to become specific. You can be ready to answer the question, "Why should I join a church?" If the outsiders are praying, loving believers, what congregation should they explore? The obvious answer is the church that best "fits" them — and will help them. Will a certain church help them better to benefit themselves, others, and God? This is where all your previous discussion of the church in general will supply the clues.

Because you, through the "outsider witnessing" process, know your prospective member, you can "zero in" on the best approach. There are some reasons for joining a church that help make life complete. If you know of key milestones in the life of any outsider, you can bring up the church's benefits through the baptism of both children and adults; of the sanctification of the marriage vows by a church wedding; and the dignity and purpose it gives at the time of death. The data suggests that a majority of the unchurched endorse these concepts. Consequently, they are an excellent means to initially interest an outsider in becoming a church member.

In getting outsiders into a church membership, there is a conviction that must be overcome. It is shown that most outsiders feel that the church places itself between Christ and the individual. They seem convinced that the individual is required to "knuckle under" to a human creed before they can gain Christ's salvation. In the majority of cases, the unchurched already believe in the divinity of Christ. What more, they feel, should the Christian church ask? They rebel at the thought that they have to dilute their individual faith with the demands of a third party — the church. They have a point.

There needs to be a great reconciliation. Outsiders must be afforded the opportunity to reconcile their faith with the demands of the church they wish to join. The outsider and the particular church must find some essential common ground on which both can establish a relationship. Most outsiders are not all that rigid in their beliefs. Sadly, many church denominations are inflexible in their creedal stance. Fortunately, there are denominations and then there are other denominations. Your challenge is to help find an outsider and a Christian denomination that can live with each other.

You can have plenty of ammunition in your discussions on the value of joining any particular church. Here's some background you'll find worth tucking away in your mind:

1. The church does not place itself between God and the believer concerning salvation. Indeed, every church's major goal is to bring the individual to a close relationship with God. What gets in the way are creedal interpretations of less important concepts. Denominational interpretations differ on matters relating to baptism, Communion, worship services, music, saving faith, good works, social activism, and a host of other more minor concerns. In free America, it is possible for any of the unchurched to find a church "home." It takes a little doing, that's granted, but the rewards are enormous.

2. The church rightly claims that it has had centuries of serving and helping individuals. Since biblical times, the church has brought faith, hope, and love to billions of individuals. It holds forth this record to the unchurched individual trying to reach a decision to join. Going it "on your own" is acceptable to God, according to the Scripture, but assembling is also endorsed and has other advantages to the individual. It is strongly urged in Scripture.

Your witness to the unchurched to join up can truthfully promise opportunity to: worship in spiritual surroundings, listen to inspirational messages, enjoy sacred music, participate in fellowship with others of similar spiritual persuasion, spiritually school your children, be constantly encouraged and refreshed, engage in rewarding work. Above all, through the church, you can promise a part in glorifying and enjoying God in ways impossible to the lone individual.

3. While many of the unchurched substantially help their neighbors, the church aids in bringing world-wide opportunities. No single individual could scour the world, as does the organized church, to "zero in" on "neighbors" most in need. As you help, through the church, your help is maximized. It

is likewise impossible for the individual, in most cases, to finance the huge sums needed to help world-neighbors. Massive food assistance, medicines, hospitals, physicians, farm aid, and other critical needs bring the Gospel to huge populations. There seems no more satisfactory way for the average person to obey the commandment, "Love Thy Neighbor," than through the operation of the church and its related organizations.

4. Try as the individual will, it is far beyond reach to receive the continual spiritual blessings available to members of the organized church. Some great "loners" have achieved mountain-top experiences in their private lives. However, the average person benefits by the help of a Godly congregation.

Only in an assembly of believers will the individual find multiple encouragements from staff and fellow members. Here, if wanted, is a rich menu of sermons, Christian education classes, special dinners, programs of all varieties, and retreats. Among the congregation is usually found a special Christian (perhaps two or three) with whom the individual can bare his or her soul.

5. It would be hard for the unchurched, unless they lived in a large city, to have available at no charge, all the inspirational literature loaned out by church libraries. The bigger the congregation, the biggerr the library. Few churches, regardless of size, do not have some form of library. The office of the minister of even the smallest church is likely to stock a number of excellent religious books ready for loan to its members.

The minister of the church, who usually is well read, provides valuable help. Whatever the subject of interest, its location can be pin-pointed. For the most recent member to the oldest sheep of the flock, the church library is a big plus.

6. Those outside the church yearn for, but seldom admit, the need for qualified, personal counseling. Even a minister of the smallest congregation helps with confidential counseling. Larger churches use, in addition to their senior pastor,

assistant pastors specializing in this work. Other large churches have Ministers of Visitation whose primary responsibility is to counsel away from the church. The largest of churches employ Christian psychologists or psychiatrists for additional mental or spiritual assistance.

Your witness to the unchurched can underscore how comforting it is to have the minister or co-worker give support:
when baptism is wanted
when making the marriage decision
when marital troubles occur
when children get into trouble
when family disruptions break out
when serious illness threatens
when convalescing is prolonged
when a death occurs
when depression develops
whenever a friend is needed
when faith, hope, and love need encouragement
when celebration is in order

There are many other benefits, some of which may hold even more importance than those listed. What does all this cost? Nothing.

There is one warning, however, which in fairness should be given. As a member becomes increasingly involved in the affairs of the church, and experiences an expanding relationship with God and Christ, there develops a desire to give. You should witness to the fact that many of those who tithe are looking for ways to give even more. Neither God, nor church, demands you give a specific amount — it's all up to you. Individualism is not lost when the unchurched joins up — rather, individualism is given the greatest opportunity to express itself. This expression brings joys and satisfactions.

The benefits of church membership come, not from a sense

of duty, but a desire to love. The minister, the staff, the officers, the members live to care and share. Some non-members complain that the church is not friendly. To be sure, some are more friendly than others because of their location, heritage, and denominational characteristics. There are differences in the outward show of friendliness between Episcopalians and Baptists; between Lutherans and Pentecostals; between Primitives and Presbyterians.

The important fact still exists. It is that the unchurched have the right, and freedom, to select that denomination that most closely shares their personal preferences. The privilege of choosing an "acceptable" type of friendliness lies within the individual. He or she, can choose any church, with just the right type of friendliness to suit their needs.

As you witness to the unchurched, you have an influence of enormous importance. Your low-key, rational discussion of the values of church membership will be more than disarming. It will be convincing. It will lead to action. It will be blessed by the presence of the Holy Spirit.

As a final plus, in any discussion to the outsider, use the example of your own life. Tell how your church membership helped you find goals, purpose, and meaning in life. Do this truthfully, without exaggeration. The unchurched are fed up with the overstatements of fanatics. If it were not so, they would have long ago become church members. Speak from your heart — admit the failures — share the successes. Be a gentle witness for the church — your way. This is why God created only one of you!

Chapter 10

You'll Never Witness Alone

Isn't it wonderful to know that wherever, whenever, or however — you never have to witness alone! He just won't allow it. The Comforter, the Counselor, the all-powerful Holy Spirit is right at your elbow. Actually, he's so close that you and he are one.

He'll help you think, help you act, help you talk. He is your guarantee that your word, attitude, and deed will not return void. At his pleasure, he will work in the lives of those to whom you witness. All you have to do is sow the seeds of your love and God's love — the Spirit will plant, cultivate, water, nourish, and cause it to grow.

If you are nervous about witnessing, this knowledge will calm you. You are important — indeed you are — but what happens is all in the hands of the third person of the Trinity. Remember that he said whenever two or more persons are gathered in his name, he is present. And, just what do you think he's doing there? Like his name implies: he's there to counsel; he's there to comfort; he's there to redeem. What a partner!

The sense of being all alone when witnessing is common. You may discuss a Christian concept and feel like you're way off base. You sense that nobody else agrees with you. It is reassuring to realize that society, not Christianity, is at fault. You know what's right with God — even though the world blinks at it. So, let the world stumble on — the Holy Spirit will assure you that the Scriptures stand. If you feel lonely, it just "ain't so." You have support.

Some deeds fall into a similar category. Perhaps it's something small, like helping a street-person to a good meal. You'll get the stares of those trying to put you down as a simpleton — as a "soft touch." Perhaps even the waitress will try to discourage you. It's easy to feel lonely, to feel out of step, in these circumstances. Push these feelings out of your mind. Get your inner strength and peace by realizing that the Holy Spirit is right with you. He's probably smiling and saying, "That's a good deed, feel good about it, forgive the critics, they know not what they do!"

Sometimes we say things we wish we hadn't. It's only human. In trying to witness by words, the right ones don't always come. So many times you'll run over what you said and feel like kicking yourself. You'll "zero in" on some inappropriate remark or slip of the tongue. If it's any consolation, the best of ministers, lecturers, evangelists have these same misgivings. And, when they make a "boo-boo," it's a dandy. It may be witnessed by millions of people! Chalk it up to being a human and don't dwell on it.

Remarkably good things have resulted from mistakes. In the area of invention, many discoveries have been the result of errors in the procedure. Your creative witnessing could fall into the same category. While something you said seemed to be a gross error, who are you to pass judgment? Perhaps for reasons beyond reasoning, you were permitted this error by the Holy Spirit. Little do you know how it will be used. He will never let you know exactly how you are communicating. You can never be sure when you say "black is not white," precisely how this is interpreted. So, don't fret it — trust him.

While accuracy is a must in witnessing, total accuracy is an impossibility. Words, attitudes, and deeds reflect not only facts, but feelings. Feelings, observations, judgments — all involved in witnessing — are beyond control. You might say, "I dearly love my wife," but this would mean different things to different people. In the vast world of feelings and opinions, leeway in interpretation makes totally accurate communications a goal, not a reality.

There are some absolutes in the Scripture which defy misinterpretation. But, they are few. And, what is "misinterpretation" to one person is "insight" to another. Whether you take Scripture literally — word for word — or simply as divinely inspired, there can be different meanings drawn from it. The semantics of Scripture is a monumental study in itself. The important matter is the meaning planted in the heart of the reader by the Holy Spirit. You have little control over this.

To have the knowledge that the Holy Spirit is helping you in your witness can bring confidence. You are about the Lord's work. He is guiding the very selection of your thoughts and words. Whatever you decide is not your decision alone. You are part of a team, and you have an unseen captain who is all-powerful. Some Christians have difficulty in accepting the idea that the Holy Spirit is present with them — here and now. There is no seeing, no hearing, no conversation. Fight these feelings with faith. God gave the Holy Spirit to counsel and comfort you. Let the Holy Spirit lead you. Listen for his leading in prayer. Meditate. Search. Examine your heart.

It is the Holy Spirit who gives power to your witness. In your witnessing, God's plan for your life, and his plan for others, come together in divine purpose. His will be done. Beyond all our intelligence and abilities is the will of God. It is the very meaning of life. It is life.

Your gentle witness will bring you into touch with God. What magnificent meaning it can give to all your days. You will become a helpmate to Christ. Now. And forever.